The Ulti.

Air Fryer Cookbook

120 Quick, Easy, And Delicious Air Frying Recipes for Your Air Fryer Cooking at Home, Hotel Or Anywhere

By Olivia Fisher

Table Of Contents

Introduction

When we want to stay fit and healthy, often the first thing we get rid of is processed food. But research has found that for most of us it will be impossible to live a junk-free life forever. So our only options:

A: giving up?

B: yo-yo dieting?

Of course not! With modern technology we can now make food at home in much healthier ways. These new gadgets reduce the oil, salts, and sugars in our foods, making them much healthier. But they also ensure we get the flavour and texture we love.

In this book we are exploring one of the best fat-cutting kitchen gadgets out there: the air fryer. An air fryer lets you recreate the taste and texture of fried foods with little to no oil. But how does it do this? Is it safe? And what, exactly, can we cook in an air fryer? Read on to find out.

Chapter 1: Everything about Air Fryers.

When it comes to discovering new and amazing kitchen gadgets, we need to understand how they work to make the most use of them. And an air fryer can be one of the most amazing kitchen gadgets you will ever try, so long as you know how to use it right. In this chapter we will explore what makes an air fryer work, which air fryers are the best ones on the market right now, what are the advantages to using an air fryer, and how to keep it working as it should. We will also investigate common questions people have about air fryers, and how an air fryer can fit into different diets.

What Is An Air Fryer?

An air fryer is a device which, as the name suggests, fries your food using air. Not exclusively air, of course, but the air is definitely a key component. In an air fryer hot air is spun incredibly fast using a fan, which makes this heat spread across our food. The end result is that we only need a teeny tiny amount of oil to get the same amazing crispiness we normally only get from a deep fry.

How Air Frying Works

Air frying is designed to create the Maillard reaction. The Maillard reaction is, in simple terms, when food browns. Contrary to popular belief, browning, and burning are not the same thing. When we cook food we have four distinct steps:

1: Cooking down. The loosening of fats, proteins, and fibres. This process dissolves fat, stretches proteins, and breaks fibres, turning the complex cells into simple fats, isolated protein, and simple sugars. This is much like what we do when we digest food, and can be created by salting foods, or by cooking them "sous vide" or in a slow cooker.

2: The Maillard reaction. This is when the food is heated enough to cause a chemical reaction between proteins and sugars, which gives us that rich, meaty, "cooked" taste we can all recognize. S'mores, the crust on breads, and the seared surface of a steak are all examples of the Maillard reaction.

3: Caramelization. This is when the sugars in a food burn, but nothing else does. Burnt sugar releases all that sweet flavour, so even though it has gone black, it just tastes strongly sweet. Brown onions, grilled grapefruit, and even the brown bits on melted cheese are great examples of caramelized sugars.

4: True burning. This is when the fats melt away, the protein and sugars dry out, and all we're left with are carbon atoms. This gives us something dry, bitter, and distinctly burnt. Some people like a bit of burnt taste on foods, such as char grilled meats, or blackened toast. But nobody likes completely burnt food, and it is even considered bad for our health.

In normal frying, the Maillard reaction happens on the outside of the food, with the inside simply being lightly cooked, as in step one. This is created by getting a large amount of oil to a very high temperature. This is because, without special gadgets, hot oil is the fastest, most efficient way to create the Maillard reaction on the surface of a food without drying out or undercooking the middle of it. However, this process comes with a serious downside: the oil.

Using so much oil in our food adds fats and calories, increases the amount of AGEs (see below) in our food, and is messy, dangerous, and expensive. An air fryer skips all those problems by replacing the tank of hot oil with a load of hot air, which heats up a thin layer of oil on our food, producing the same reaction in a much better way.

The Advantages Of Using An Air Fryer

There are many advantages to using an air fryer. **First of all, it massively reduces the amount of fats in your food compared to any other method of frying.** When we fry foods fats tend to soak into them, so the less fat around your food, the less fat in your food. And even if you're not worried about fats in and of themselves, it is worth remembering that the fats in fried foods are more than just fat. Typically, they are vegetable oils, high in inflammatory omega 6 oils, and loaded with calories. So by reducing the fat in your fried food, you are also reducing the amount of processed food, inflammatory food, and calories in your diet.

Secondly, an air fryer is much more economical and clean than a deep fat fryer.

When you use a deep fat fryer you need to change the oil after every few hours of use. This could mean you change it every time you use it, or you change it every couple of days. But either way, that's a few gallons of oil you are throwing away, and a whole deep fat fryer you are cleaning, for just a few servings of fries. On the other hand, an air fryer uses just a thin layer of oil, saving much money, and is much less greasy and messy to clean.

Thirdly, an air fryer is much safer than almost any other conventional method of frying. Hot oil is incredibly dangerous, but most frying methods have us getting our skin very close to the oil, which is always risky. But an air fryer is much safer. We just put our lightly oiled foods into it and close the lid, locking everything safely away inside. Because the cooking is timed, and it is very hard to overcook something in the air fryer, we do not need to open it and expose ourselves to the heat. And because it is sealed, we know that our families, pets, and even ourselves are safe from splattering or spilling hot oil.

Fourthly, air frying reduces the amount of AGEs in our foods. An AGE is an Advanced Glycation End-product. This is what happens when proteins, fats, and sugars begin to burn and blend together, which is what we see with direct heat cooking such as pan-frying or grilling. AGEs have been linked to increased immune system problems, increased risk of cancer, and worse ageing. An air fryer can therefore be considered a great step towards cooking healthier foods.

Finally, air frying delivers some seriously satisfying crispy results. There is something just amazing about biting into a food that is delightfully crispy, which is why so many of the snacks we love are crunchy. Chips, fries, cookies, pastry, scratchings, nuts, chocolate... That crunch or crackle is irresistible. And when we can replace our unhealthy packaged foods with an equally satisfying healthy crunch, we are a step closer to being healthy and happy.

Choosing An Air Fryer

All air fryers will cook your food by blasting extremely hot air over some lightly oiled food. But there are some key differences between the air fryers available on the market right now that could sway your decision to buy one over another.

Most air fryers come with adjustable temperatures and timers, letting you cook food very precisely. Although there are some available which do not have these features, I would not recommend using them, as they can be more trouble than they are worth.

Most air fryers will come with a few options in terms of baskets and stands. Again, it is not worth getting one that only has one basket or way of cooking. Try and get one with a few different options, or which you can get special inserts for. This will make your air fryer cooking more varied and interesting.

Some air fryers are very compact, whereas others take up as much counter room as a slow cooker or a microwave! Usually the bigger ones have more functions, and the smallest ones have almost no variety. Depending on the space you have, you might need to sacrifice a bit of space or a bit of variety to get the right air fryer for you.

Some air fryers include sophisticated timers with settings for different foods and auto shut-offs for when the fryer gets too hot, too dry, or the food is done. These are usually well worth the investment as they are even easier and safer to use.

A double or triple layer rack is a great addition to any air fryer. This sort of rack literally multiplies the amount of food you can cook, making it much quicker and easier to make a meal for the family, or to cook in bulk.

Air Fryer FAQs

1. Can I cook a variety of foods in an air fryer?
Yes you can. Many people think it is just for fries and deep-fried foods like corndogs, but in reality you can use an air fryer to cook almost anything you like. You can even use it to bake flat breads and cakes, and to grill things!

2. Is an air fryer dangerous?
Far from it! Air fryers are much safer than conventional frying methods, as there is less oil and the heat is safely contained in the gadget. Like with all electronic kitchen equipment, there is the slight risk of an electrical fault or overheating. But the fryer will include fuses and even auto shut-off options, making it no more dangerous than, for example, a hair drier.

3. Can I use parchment paper or tin foil in my air fryer?
Yes, you can. As the air fryer is not a dry environment, there is no risk of burning. Just

make sure that you do not completely seal off any area, though, as they hot air needs to move freely!

4. Can I use my air fryer without any oil?

You can, but it's not really recommended. You need a little oil covering your food to create the reaction and get that perfect "fried" taste. Otherwise your food is just going to be dry on the outside and soft on the inside, not truly crispy.

5. How long will my air fryer take to cook my food?

Always consult the manual first, but typically an air fryer will take anywhere from 5 to 60 minutes to cook a full load of food to crispy perfection.

6. How much food can I cook in my air fryer?

It really depends on your fryer, so make sure to check the manual. But typically your air fryer will have three restrictions: weight, depth, and space. You can tell the weight restriction by reading the manual. You can tell the depth restriction by reading the manual or checking the basket for a "max" line. And when it comes to space, always make sure there are gaps between the items you are trying to fry. The oil and hot air needs to completely cover your food, otherwise it will not get crisp, so make sure the air can flow all around every single piece in the fryer.

7. Can I cook food from frozen in my air fryer?

Absolutely! In fact, air fryers are particularly good for cooking food like chips, croquettes, and fried chicken from frozen. The combination of the light frying that manufacturers do before freezing and the air fryer's second frying makes frozen foods ridiculously crispy and tasty. It really upgrades your "oven" fries!

8. How is an air fryer different from a convection oven?

An air fryer and a convection oven are similar in that they both use hot air to cook food, but that's about it. The hot air in your air fryer moves much faster and the heat is more evenly distributed than in a convection oven. Your air fryer is much smaller than a convection oven, too. Because of these differences air fryers cook a wider variety of food, and cook much faster, than convection ovens.

9. Will the food taste exactly like deep fried food?

Nothing will really taste like deep fried food except deep fried food. This is because you can't take all that oil out of a food and make it taste like it's still full of oil. However, an air fryer creates the desirable Maillard reaction taste for very little oil, making it the healthy version of deep frying.

10. Could I use an air fryer in my student accommodation or hotel?
Yes, you can. An air fryer does not have an open heat source, like a grill or a stove would. This means it meets the fire safety requirements of a student room or a hotel room, so you can use it freely.

Air Frying On Different Diets

Air frying is not just for low fat dieters, it is for everyone.

On a **low fat diet (LF)**, it allows you to reduce the amount of oil in your food whilst enjoying your usual treats. By using only a little bit of oil you can get that satisfying crunch without eating too much fat, or too many calories.

On a **low carb diet (LC)**, it lets you get the satisfaction of a crunchy snack without resorting to grains or potatoes. This also makes it great for variants of the low carb diet, such as the **ketogenic diet (KD)** or the **Atkins diet (AK)**.

On a whole foods diet it lets you control the type and amount of oil you are using. The sort of oil we normally cook with when frying is highly allergenic vegetable oils, loaded with omega 6 fatty acids and low in nutrition. But healthy alternatives typically do not handle deep frying well, or are expensive. By using only a little oil, we make it cheap and easy to enjoy fried food on a **Paleo diet (PL)** or a **whole foods diet (WD)**.

On a **high protein diet (HP)**, it adds options to our menu without sacrificing health. We can enjoy different versions of fried and grilled proteins without eating extra AGEs.

On a **vegan (VGN)**, **vegetarian (VGI)**, or **pescetarian diet (PD)**, it allows you to know exactly what is going into your junk food, ensuring that it is healthy and ethical at once.

Chapter 2: Air Frying 101

So, now we know what our air fryer is, what it does, and what sort of a one we want to get, we need to think about how we are using it. Many people get stuck using their air fryer just for fries and frozen croquettes, or not using it at all. But that is a bit sad, because an air fryer can be so versatile if you work hard to find different ways of using it. In this chapter we will see how we can make great daily use of our air fryer.

How To Air Fry Almost Anything

When it comes to air frying we need to remember that anything can be cooked this way, as long as we prepare it properly. **First, when cooking from frozen, anything you air fry needs a nice, light coating of oil.** You can achieve this by tossing your food in a bowl or strainer with a little oil, or by placing it on the rack and drizzling oil over it, or drizzling oil along the bottom of the air fryer, it will give a crispiness along with avoiding sticking to the bottom of the fryer. You can also use a one calorie spray oil, for a thin and even coating.

Next, you need to make sure you don't overfill your air fryer. Check the weight limit and the max line, but above all check how your food looks! If the food looks super crowded in there, you will need to thin it out and give it some space. And if after cooking you find everything isn't as crisp as you would like, you might need to give it another shake, another spray of oil, and cook it at super high temperature for a few more minutes.

Finally, it is better to go too quick and hot than too low and slow. Start on the lowest number of minutes and the highest temperature, and then adjust the time up and the temperature from there. This is because crispiness comes from high heats, but high heats are not sustainable for a long amount of time. If you want a perfectly crispy exterior and a perfectly cooked inside, you need to find that balance of heat and time where the temperature penetrates the food to its core, but also dries and crisps the outside of the food. In this book you will practise your timing skills until you can cook almost anything in an air fryer.

In chapters 3-10 we will go into more detail about how to cook a wide range of foods in our air fryer. So be ready to get creative and have a great time cooking healthy, tasty food.

Your Air Fryer Accessories

Your air fryer comes with four distinct parts, and there are even some additional extras, or alternative versions of the main parts, which you need to be familiar with before you start cooking. The four main bits are the body of the fryer, the drawer, the basket, and the rack. Your food will go in the basket. The main body and the drawer are there to reflect heat well and to make the fryer easy to clean. The rack is there to avoid the food from coming in direct contact with a heat source.

You can get different types of mesh baskets for different volumes of food. You can also get multi-level racks which let you cook with two or more different baskets at a time. Always remember that because of how air fryers work there will be a transfer of air and oil between the baskets. This means that taste and scents will transfer from food to food. It also means that if you cook an allergenic food in one basket, the foods in the other baskets will be contaminated.

You can get dividers if you want to air fry two different foods in the same basket and keep them sort of separate. However, there isn't really much of a point to doing this. As I said, due to the way air frying works the scents and tastes of the different foods will transfer into each other anyway. So stopping the foods from touching one another doesn't do anything at all.

You can get baking dishes for your air fryer. These make a fantastic addition because they massively improve the range of foods you can cook in your air fryer. There are some standard baking trays which may fit in an air fryer, but you would be running the risk of restricting air flow, which could damage your air fryer. So it's a smart idea to invest in a non-stick air fryer baking dish. In this category you can get deep baking dishes for cakes, cupcake dishes, and pizza pans, depending on your air fryer baking needs.

Next, you can get extra grill racks, including kebab skewer racks. These let you cook your own healthy version of barbecue foods in your air fryer, using only a little oil and a lot of hot air. The removal of a direct heat source and an open flame means the char is completely gone. This might be a deal breaker for some people, but it also makes your grilled foods many times healthier, because AGE production is restricted.

You can also use small ramekins for steaming and stewing liquid foods, and for frying runny foods such as eggs and cheeses. This is because you cannot let too much fluid drip into the main drawer of the air fryer, so you need something to contain excess juices. If you do use a ramekin make sure that it is small enough that the air can move around and over it.

Finally, you can get steamer liners, if you want to steam or bake in your air fryer with minimal mess. These are perfect if you will be steaming dumplings or cooking something gooey and cheesy on your air fryer grill, but you don't really need the special liners. Cutting the right size and shape of baking paper will do the same job for a lot less money.

How To Clean Your Air Fryer

Cleaning an air fryer is much quicker and easier than cleaning any deep fat fryer or dehydrator. Simple take the pan and basket out of the air fryer and add hot water and a little dish soap. Let them soak for 10-30 minutes. Add a bit more warm water and gently wipe clean with a cloth or non-abrasive brush. You can also put these parts directly in your dishwasher.

To clean the inside of your fryer, use hot water only and a soft sponge or cloth. Gently wipe in circles to remove any grease or residue. If there is food residue struck, you can use hotter water or a soft bristle brush. I actually find a toothbrush works best! Don't use a harsh brush or a steel wire brush as these will damage the non-stick coating and the heating parts of your air fryer. Make sure after cleaning the inside that you pat it dry with paper towels or a no-fuzz duster. Always check behind for leftover fluff or paper before you use it again.

The outside of your air fryer will not develop a coating of greasy oil, unlike a deep fat fryer, so you don't need to clean it as often as the pan. A gentle wipe down with a dust cloth should keep it free of dust and debris. If you get any sauce or grease on the outside, use a moist cloth with a tiny bit of washing up liquid to wipe the outside gently clean.

If an air fryer has not been cleaned for a long time sometimes a layer of grease can build up. For this, mix a spray bottle with warm water and baking powder and lightly spray everything. Then brush it down with a soft or medium bristle brush. You may need to do this a few times to clean the air fryer thoroughly.

How To Care For Your Air Fryer

Caring for your air fryer is as simple as cleaning it after every use and putting a cover on it to keep dust out when you are not using it. Keep an eye out for:
- Bad smells.
- White smoke.
- Burning smells.
- Hot spots on your food.
- Dripping grease.

As long as you are cleaning it regularly, keeping it covered and dry, and not noticing any strange signs coming from it, everything should be fine.

Staying Safe When Air Frying

However safe an appliance is, there are always things that can happen which would make it unsafe. Therefore, we need to try and remember to look after our air fryer properly and always follow manufacturer guidelines when using it. That said, there are some universal precautions we need to take when using an air fryer.

1. Never wash the electrical or heating components under water. Mixing electricity and water is always dangerous. When you clean the electrical and heating elements, make sure to lightly wipe them with a damp, but not a dripping wet cloth. And make sure the air fryer is dry before using it next.
2. Never fill the pan with oil. This is not a deep fat fryer and is not designed to hold a pile of oil. Best case scenario your air fryer will just break. Worst case scenario you risk electrocution and explosions of hot oil.
3. Never open your air fryer when it has reached full temperature. Some air fryers allow you to pull the drawer out to add more food as you go, but most are not safe to open once the peak temperature has been reached. The inside can be as hot as 400F, so be very careful.

4. Never touch the insides of the fryer until it has been allowed to cool. Again, they could be at 400F. Wait until it's cooled to clean inside.

5. Never leave children, pets, or vulnerable people unattended near your air fryer. This is still an electric gadget and has very hot parts, making it unsafe for vulnerable people and animals.

6. Never put anything on top of your air fryer. This could damage the top of it, or cause it to overheat, both of which can break it.

7. Always keep your power chord away from heated surfaces. A power chord that gets hot is at risk of melting or starting an electric fire, so make sure it is behind your fryer and away from heat.

8. Always put your air fryer on an even surface. This is to stop it from falling or leaking, both of which could prove dangerous.

9. Always keep your air fryer clean. As it uses high temperatures a dirty air fryer could potentially start a grease fire.

10. Always use your warranty. If your air fryer stops working, do not try and fix it yourself or get an unqualified person to do so. This could make it dangerous and void your warranty. Instead, call the manufacturer and get a certified repairman to fix it for you.

11. Always read the manual. Some of these points may not apply to your air fryer, such as point 3, which does not apply to some models. And some things not mentioned here might be important for your air fryer. Always be careful and read the manual front to back.

Tips And Mistakes

To make the most out of your air fryer and to avoid common mistakes, consider the following tips:

1. Cook using traditional oils and high-temperature fats. Sunflower oil, peanut oil, vegetable oil, coconut oil, lard, and tallow all withstand high temperatures well.

2. Use an oil spray, or put your oil in a clean spray bottle, to get an even, light mist of cooking oil on your food.

3. To add spices to your foods, mix the oils and spices into a paste or a seasoned oil and allow to soak for 2-24 hours.

4. Don't bother with oil if you are cooking/ using frozen, oven-bake ingredients such as oven fries, as these come with a little oil in the first place.

5. If your ingredients touch you will need to pause your cooking halfway through

to shake the basket. This helps separate foods that are sticking together, and makes sure you get an even, crispy coating.

6. If your basket cannot be removed during cooking, cook your foods in two parts.
7. If you are looking for something golden brown, your air fryer may not be able to deliver that colouring. Consider using ready-to-bake frozen foods for a brown look.
8. If you want your vegetables to be crispy you will need to bread them with an oil-based crumb, pastry, or batter coating.
9. Make sure your food is completely dry before spraying oil, so that the oil sticks.
10. With an air fryer only a little oil is needed. So if you cook a very fatty food, it will probably not crisp up.

Notes On Recipes

The next chapters of the book will show you a variety of amazing recipes to try in your air fryer. Each recipe comes in the same format. First we have a title which tells us what kind of a recipe it is. Then we have the number of servings, prep time, and cooking time, and temperature for this amount.

The temperature guidelines:
Low is 300 - 325F.
Medium is 325 - 350F.
High is 350 - 400F.

The following is a list of diets it is suitable for:
HP, means High Protein Diet and a food qualifies if it has 20g or more of protein.
KD, means Ketogenic Diet and a food counts if it has under 10g of carbs.
LC, means Low Carb Diet and a food counts if it has under 40g of carbs.
LF, means Low Fat Diet and a food counts if it has under 10g of fat.
AK, means Atkins Diet and a food counts if 20% or fewer of its calories come from carbs.
PL, means Paleo or Primal Diet and a food counts it if has no grains, pulses, dairy, or processed foods.
VGI, means Vegetarian Diet and a food counts if it has no meat or fish.
VGN, means Vegan Diet and a food counts if it has no animal products at all.
PC, means Pescetarian Diet and a food counts if it has no red meat, but includes fish and/or eggs or dairy.

WD, means Whole Foods Diet and a food qualifies if it is made entirely from scratch out of fresh foods.

Next, we get to the recipes. We will have a list of ingredients, as well as any alternatives we could use to make the meal suitable for other diets. And then we have the instructions which, given how quick and easy an air fryer is to use, will be very brief.

Finally, we have the nutritional values per serving of the meal. This will tell us how many calories, as well as grams of net carbs, protein, and fats that can be found in each portion of the meal. Below will be a serving suggestion.

As air fried food can sometimes be complete in and of itself, or sometimes will be a component of a larger meal, the nutritional guidelines laid out will refer only to the food made using the ingredients in the list. So if, for example, there is a salad included in the recipe, then that salad is part of the meal and its ingredients and nutritional values are included in the recipe. But if the salad is mentioned below the recipe, then the salad ingredients have not been included in the nutritional information.

Oil. When oil is mentioned in a recipe, please note that a light drizzle, coating, a few tablespoons will enhance the crisping technique. There is no need to saturate your food in oil to achieve a crisp texture.

Chapter 3: Breakfast & Brunch

Breakfast is the most important meal of the day. It gives us the energy we need to keep going, and makes for a great excuse for the family to get together before heading out for the day. But all too often when we think of a cooked breakfast we think of fried food: fried eggs, fried bacon, deep fried hash browns. With an air fryer we can make delectable "fried" breakfasts that are still healthy for us.

Air Fried Maple Bacon.

Serves 4. Prep time: 2 minutes. Cooking: 10 minutes on medium.
Suitable for: KD, LC, AK, PL, WD.

Ingredients:
- 12 slices back bacon
- 1Tbsp maple syrup
- oil

Directions:
1. Pat your bacon dry. Toss it with the maple syrup.
2. Drizzle oil over bottom of air fryer. Place bacon in your air fryer. Cook at 325F for 10 minutes.

Nutritional values per serving: KCAL: 150; net C 2g; P 12g; F 23g.
Serve with any other combination of breakfast foods.

Air Fried Eggs.

Serves 4. Prep time: 5 minutes. Cooking: 10 minutes on medium.
Suitable for: HP, KD, LC, AK, PL, VGI, PC, WD.

Ingredients:
- 8 eggs
- few drops oil

Directions:
1. Spray four small ramekins with oil.
2. Crack two eggs into each ramekin.
3. Place in air fryer. Cook at 325F for 10 minutes.

Nutritional values per serving: KCAL: 220; net C 0g; P 40g; F 10g.
Serve with any other combination of breakfast foods.

Air Fried Hash Browns.

Serves 4. Prep time: 10 minutes. Cooking: 15 minutes on high.
Suitable for: LF, VGI, VGN, PC, WD.

Ingredients:
- 2 cups grated potatoes
- 2 eggs, beaten
- 1 Tbsp oil
- 1 Tbsp sweet paprika
- salt and pepper to taste

Directions:
1. In a bowl, combine the oil, paprika, salt and pepper. Leave for 2 hours.
2. Grate the potatoes. Pat them dry thoroughly.
3. Mix in the beaten eggs.
4. Form four patties. Spray with oil.
5. Place in a grill pan in you air fryer. Cook at 400F for 15 minutes.

Nutritional values per serving: KCAL: 200; net C 40g; P 4g; F 5g.
Serve with any other combination of breakfast foods.

Air Fried French Toast.

Serves 4. Prep time: 20 minutes. Cooking: 40 minutes on high.
Suitable for: LF, VGI, PC.

Ingredients:
- 4 thick slices or 8 normal slices of bread
- 1 Tbsp milk
- 3 eggs, beaten
- 1 Tbsp oil

Directions:
1. Whisk the eggs. Add the milk. Stir well.
2. Soak the bread in the egg mixture.
3. Drizzle oil over bottom of air fryer.
4. Place bread in air fryer. Cook at 350F for 5 minutes, per side.

Nutritional values per serving: KCAL: 280; net C 45g; P 10g; F 9g.
Serve with fresh fruit, or other breakfast foods.

Air Fried Battered Mushrooms.

Serves 8. Prep time: 14 minutes. Cooking: 5 minutes on high.
Suitable for: LC, LF, AK, VGI, VGN, PC, WD.

Ingredients:
- 1 cup flour
- 4 Tbsp oil
- 1 egg, beaten
- 2 cups button mushrooms, washed and dried

- salt and pepper to taste

Directions:
1. In a bowl, mix the flour and seasonings.
2. Dip the mushrooms in the flour, the egg, and then the breadcrumbs.
3. Drizzle oil over the bottom of the air fryer.
4. Cook in air fryer at 350F for 5 minutes. If you prefer a crispier mushroom, cook on other side for 2 minutes.

Nutritional values per serving: KCAL: 50; net C 10g; P 2g; F 4g.
Serve with side of eggs.

Air Fried Chicken & Waffles.

Serves 4. Prep time: 10 minutes. Cooking: 36 minutes on medium.
Suitable for: HP, LC, LF.

Ingredients:
- 1 cup flour
- 4 eggs, beaten
- 1 cup buttermilk
- 6 Tbsp oil
- herbes du provence
- salt and pepper
- 4 chicken breasts
- 4 frozen waffles

Directions:
1. In a bowl, combine the flour and herbes, salt, and pepper.
2. Rinse the chicken, pat dry.
3. In a large baggie, pour in the buttermilk. Add the chicken. Massage the buttermilk into the chicken, through the baggie. Marinate in fridge for 20 minutes to 2 hours.
4. Once marinating completed, dip the chicken in seasoned flour, then egg mixture, and then the breadcrumbs.

5. Drizzle oil over bottom of your air fryer.
6. Cook chicken at 325F for 18 minutes. Cook waffle at 325F for 4 minutes.
7. When plating, place a waffle down, then chicken on top. Drizzle maple syrup over both.

Nutritional values per serving: KCAL: 320; net C 37g; P 35g; F 7g.
Serve with maple syrup.

Air Fried Sausages.

Serves 4. Prep time: 2 minutes. Cooking: 10 minutes on medium.
Suitable for: HP, KD, LC, LF, AK, PL, WD.

Ingredients:
- 8 low fat, no crumb frankfurter sausages
- 1 Tbsp oil

Directions:
1. Spiral cut or hasselback the sausages.
2. Drizzle oil over bottom of your air fryer.
3. Cook at 340F for 10 minutes.

Nutritional values per serving: KCAL: 200; net C 4g; P 45g; F 7g.
Serve with any other combination of breakfast foods.

Air Fried Croissants.

Serves 8. Prep time: 10 minutes. Cooking: 60 minutes on high.
Suitable for: LF, VGI, VGN, PC.

Ingredients:
- 7 ounces chilled ready-made puff pastry
- 2 Tbsp milk

Directions:
1. Cut the pastry into triangles and roll up into crescent shapes.
2. Brush with milk.
3. Place in the basket, do not pile on top of each other or allow to touch!
4. Cook at 400F for 10 minutes.
5. Repeat until all the croissants are cooked.

Nutritional values per serving: KCAL: 100; net C 42g; P 3g; F 2g.
Serve with jam or any combination of breakfast foods.

Air Fried Chorizo & Beans.

Serves 4. Prep time: 5 minutes. Cooking: 20 minutes on medium.
Suitable for: HP, LC, LF, WD.

Ingredients:
- 4 chorizo sausages
- 1 can beans, your choice
- 2 Tbsp tomato paste
- 1 tsp
- Pinch of salt, and pepper

Directions:
1. Drain half the liquid from beans. Oil 4 ramekins.
2. Mix the tomato and seasonings into the beans. Divide among ramekins.
3. Make small cuts along sides of chorizo. Evenly coat the chorizo with oil.
4. Place ramekins and chorizo in air fryer. Cook everything at 325 for 20 minutes.

Nutritional values per serving: KCAL: 300; net C 34g; P 28g; F 5g.
Serve with bread and butter.

Air Fried Green Tomatoes.

Serves 8. Prep time: 20 minutes. Cooking: 80 minutes on medium.
Suitable for: LC, LF, VGI, VGN, PC, WD.

Ingredients:
- 4 green tomatoes
- 2 eggs, beaten
- 1 cup flour
- ½ cup cornmeal
- ½ cup breadcrumbs
- 2 Tbsp milk
- 1 Tbsp paprika
- 1 Tbsp garlic powder
- salt and pepper to taste
- 1 kcal spray

Directions:
1. Slice the tomatoes in ¼ inch rings.
2. Season flour with paprika, garlic powder, salt, and pepper.
3. Dip sliced tomatoes in seasoned flour, then egg mixture, then breadcrumbs.
4. Spray each slice of tomato with oil.
5. Cook at 350F for 20 minutes.
6. Repeat until all cooked.

Nutritional values per serving: KCAL: 60; net C 15g; P 4g; F 5g.
Serve with breakfast foods.

Air Fried Stuffed Croquettes.

Serves 4. Prep time: 20 minutes. Cooking: 20 minutes on high.
Suitable for: HP, LC, LF, VGI, PC, WD.

Ingredients:
- 1 cup mashed potatoes
- 1 egg, beaten
- ½ cup flour
- 2 Tbsp oil
- ¼ cup medium, or sharp cheddar cheese, cubed small
- salt and pepper to taste

Directions:
1. Mash the potatoes. Roll into bite-size pieces.
2. Press thumb into center of mash potatoe ball, insert a cheese cube. Roll until cheese is covered.
3. In a bowl, combine the flour, salt, and pepper.
4. Roll the potato balls in the seasoned flour, then egg mixture, then breadcrumbs.
5. Drizzle oil over bottom of air fryer. Cook in your air fryer at 400F for 20 minutes.

Nutritional values per serving: KCAL: 100; net C 25g; P 10g; F 5g.
Serve with any other combination of breakfast foods.

Air Fried Refried Beans.

Serves 8. Prep time: 4 minutes. Cooking: 15 minutes on high.
Suitable for: LF, VGI, VGN, PC, WD.

Ingredients:
- 2 cans pinto beans
- Mexican seasoning
- oil

Directions:
1. Mash the beans with the seasoning.
2. Drizzle oil over bottom of air fryer. Place beans in air fryer.
3. Cook at 400F for 5 minutes.
4. Open air fryer, stir the beans.
5. Cook at 400F for another 10 minutes.

Nutritional values per serving: KCAL: 100; net C 41g; P 12g; F 6g.
Serve with any other combination of breakfast foods.

Air Fried Breakfast Skewers.

Serves 4. Prep time: 12 minutes. Cooking: 10 minutes on medium.
Suitable for: HP, LC, LF, AK, PL, WD.

Ingredients:
- 4 sausages
- 4 rashers bacon
- 2 tomatoes
- 1 cup button mushrooms, stems removed
- oil
- 1 Tbsp flour

Directions:
1. Cut the food into bite-size pieces.
2. Slide ingredients onto skewers, alternating pieces. Roll the skewers in the flour.
3. Drizzle oil along bottom of air fryer. Cook at 375F for 10 minutes.

Nutritional values per serving: KCAL: 300; net C 8g; P 37g; F 7g.
Serve with breakfast foods.

Air Fried Steak And Eggs.

Serves 2. Prep time: 2 minutes. Cooking: 10 minutes on medium.
Suitable for: HP, KD, LC, AK, PL, WD.

Ingredients:
- 2 x 6ounc steaks
- 4 eggs
- 1 kcal spray
- salt and pepper to taste

Directions:
1. Spray 2 ramekins with oil.
2. Crack eggs into ramekins. Season with salt and pepper.
3. Spray both sides of steak with oil.
4. Add the ramekins and steak to air fryer. (If they don't all fit, cook steak first, allow the steak to rest and cook the eggs.)
5. Cook steak at 350F for 10 minutes. Cook eggs at 325F for 5 minutes, or until desired consistency.

Nutritional values per serving: KCAL: 400; net C 9g; P 53g; F 18g.
Serve as-is.

Air Fried Grilled Cheese.

Serves 4. Prep time: 10 minutes. Cooking: 20 minutes on high.
Suitable for: LC, VGI, PC.

Ingredients:
- 8 slices of bread
- 2 cups grated cheese
- salt and pepper to taste
- 1 kcal spray

Directions:

1. In a bowl, mix the cheese with salt and pepper.
2. Spray both sides of the bread with oil. Fill with cheese.
3. Place sandwiches in air fryer or in grill pan in air fryer. Cook at 400F for 5 minutes on one side, then 2 minutes other side.

Nutritional values per serving: *KCAL: 230; net C 30g; P 15g; F 15g.*
Serve as is.

Chapter 4: Lunch & Dinner.

Making a light, delicious lunch or dinner can be a serious challenge for many of us. Especially when we are fast-food lovers! But with an air fryer you can make quick, healthy, crunchy meals for any time of day, taking all your worries away.

Air Fried Turkey And Mushroom Burgers.

Serves 5. Prep time: 10 minutes. Cooking: 10 minutes on medium.
Suitable for: HP, KD, LC, LF, AK, PL, WD.

Ingredients:
- 1 cup fresh mushrooms, minced
- 1 pound lean ground turkey
- 1 egg, beaten
- ¼ cup breadcrumbs
- salt and pepper to taste
- 1 kcal spray

Directions:
1. In a bowl, mix the mushrooms, turkey, egg, breadcrumbs, salt and pepper.
2. Pat dry. Shape into patties.
3. Spray each side of burger with oil.
4. Place in air fryer. Cook at 375F for 10 minutes.

Nutritional values per serving: KCAL: 120; net C 7g; P 35g; F 3g.
Serve on buns with a salad.

Air Fried Traditional Meatloaf.

Serves 4. Prep time: 5 minutes. Cooking: 10 minutes on high.
Suitable for: HP, LC, LF.

Ingredients:
- 4 slices leftover meatloaf

- 1 kcal spray
- salt and pepper to taste

Directions:
1. Spray both sides of meatloaf. Season with salt and pepper.
2. Place in air fryer. Cook at 380F for 10 minutes.

Nutritional values per serving: KCAL: 300; net C 34g; P 35g; F 8g.
Serve with steamed veggies.

Air Fried Green Curry Shrimp.

Serves 6. Prep time: 60 minutes. Cooking: 25 minutes on low.
Suitable for: HP, LF, PC, WD.

Ingredients:
- 2 pounds cooked noodles; egg noodles, vermicelli, linguine, rice noodles
- 15 cooked jumbo shrimp
- 1 pound stir fry vegetables
- Thai fish sauce
- Thai green curry paste
- oil

Directions:
1. As stated above. The noodles and shrimp should be pre-cooked in your favorite method. Once they are cooled. In a large baggie, pour in the Thai fish sauce. Add the noodles and shrimp. Massage the marinade so the ingredients are coated evenly. Marinate in fridge for 20 minutes up to 2 hours.
2. Cook the vegetables in a grill pan for 5 minutes on low. Set aside.
3. Stir the Thai green curry into the noodles and shrimp. Add the vegetables to the noodles and shrimp. Massage briefly.
4. Drizzle oil over bottom of air fryer. Cook at 325F for 15 minutes.

Nutritional values per serving: KCAL: 271; net C 49g; P 23g; F 6g.
Serve with lemon or lime wedges.

Air Fried Beef Burgers.

Serves 5. Prep time: 10 minutes. Cooking: 10 minutes on medium.
Suitable for: HP, KD, LC, LF, AK, PL, WD.

Ingredients:
- 1 pound lean ground beef
- 1 egg
- ¼ cup breadcrumbs
- Dash of Worcestershire sauce
- Dash of mustard
- salt and pepper to taste
- 1 kcal spray

Directions:
1. In a bowl, mix the ground beef, egg, breadcrumbs, Worcestershire sauce, mustard, salt and pepper. Stir until mixed. Shape into 5 burger patties.
2. Pat dry. Spray both sides with oil.
3. Place in air fryer. Cook at 350F for 10 minutes.

Nutritional values per serving: KCAL: net C 5g; P 38g; F 9g.
Serve on buns with a salad.

Air Fried Shrimp Patties.

Serves 5. Prep time: 10 minutes. Cooking: 10 minutes on medium.
Suitable for: HP, KD, LC, LF, AK, PL, PC, WD.

Ingredients:
- 1 cup fresh cabbage, diced
- 1 pound diced shrimp
- 1 egg
- ¼ cup breadcrumbs
- Dash of paprika

- 1 green onion, minced
- salt and pepper to taste
- 1 kcal spray

Directions:
1. In a bowl, mix the shrimp, cabbage, egg, breadcrumbs, paprika, green onion, salt and pepper. Stir well.
2. Form the mixture into patties, around the size of inside your palm. Pat dry.
3. Spray both sides with oil. Place in air fryer.
4. Cook at 340F for 10 minutes.

Nutritional values per serving: *KCAL: 130; net C 1g; P 30g; F 2g.*
Serve on buns with a salad.

Air Fried Tofu Loaf.

Serves 4. Prep time: 5 minutes. Cooking: 10 minutes on high.
Suitable for: HP, KD, LC, LF, AK, VGI, VGN, PC.

Ingredients:
- 4 slices firm tofu
- 1 kcal spray
- salt and pepper to taste

Directions:
1. Spray your tofu with kcal spray. Season with salt and pepper.
2. Place in air fryer. Cook at 380F for 10 minutes.

Nutritional values per serving: *KCAL: 80; net C 12g; P 32g; F 6g.*
Serve with steamed veggies.

Air Fried Spicy Lamb Curry.

Serves 6. Prep time: 20 minutes. Cooking: 25 minutes on low.
Suitable for: HP, KD, LC, AK, PL, WD.

Ingredients:
- 2 pounds diced lamb
- 1 pound chopped nightshade vegetables (tomato, zucchini, eggplant, etc.)
- madras paste curry sauce
- oil

Directions:
1. In a large baggie pour in the curry sauce. Add the lamb pieces and vegetables. Massage the bag to ensure even coating. Place in fridge to marinate for 1 hour.
2. Grease ramekins with oil. Spoon lamb mixture into ramekins
3. Place in air fryer. Cook at 325F for 25 minutes.

Nutritional values per serving: KCAL: 280; net C 7g; P 42g; F 17g.
Serve with rice or naan.

Air Fried Chicken Burgers.

Serves 5. Prep time: 10 minutes. Cooking: 10 minutes on medium.
Suitable for: HP, LC, LF, WD.

Ingredients:
- 1 pound lean ground chicken breast
- 1 egg
- ¼ cup breadcrumbs
- 1 tsp dried minced onion
- 1 tsp garlic powder
- salt and pepper to taste
- 1 kcal spray

Directions:

1. In a bowl, combine the ground chicken, egg, breadcrumbs, minced onion, garlic powder, salt, and pepper. Stir well.
2. Form into patties. Pat dry.
3. Spray both sides with oil.
4. Place in air fryer. Cook at 340F for 10 minutes.

Nutritional values per serving: KCAL: net C 13g; P 32g; F 6g.
Serve on buns with a salad.

Air Fried Bean Burgers.

Serves 5. Prep time: 10 minutes. Cooking: 10 minutes on medium.
Suitable for: HP, LC, LF, VGI, VGN, PC, WD.

Ingredients:
- 2 ounces lentils, boiled, drained
- ½ pound pinto beans, boiled, drained
- ½ pound black beans, boiled, drained
- ½ bell pepper, finely chopped
- ½ white onion, finely chopped
- 1 garlic clove, finely chopped
- ¼ tsp chili powder
- ¼ tsp cumin
- 1 – 3 Tbsp chili sauce
- salt and pepper to taste
- 1 kcal spray

Directions:
1. In a bowl, mix the lentils, pinto beans, black beans. Mash with a fork.
2. Stir in the bell pepper, onion, garlic clove, chili powder, cum, salt, pepper.
3. Start with 1 tablespoon of chili sauce. Stir in more until desired consistency is reach.
4. Shape into patties. Pat dry.
5. Spray each side with oil.

6. Place in air fryer. Cook at 340F for 10 minutes.

Nutritional values per serving: KCAL: 155; net C 29g; P 21g; F 2g.
Serve on buns with a salad.

Air Fried Chicken Meatloaf.

Serves 4. Prep time: 5 minutes. Cooking: 10 minutes on high.
Suitable for: HP, LC, LF, AK.

Ingredients:
- 4 slices leftover chicken meatloaf
- 1 kcal spray
- ¼ cup flour
- salt and pepper to taste

Directions:
1. In a bowl, mix the flour with salt and pepper.
2. Spray both sides of chicken meatloaf with oil.
3. Dip the pieces in flour.
4. Place in oil fryer. Cook at 380F for 10 minutes.

Nutritional values per serving: KCAL: 210; net C 12g; P 34g; F 4g.
Serve with steamed veggies.

Air Fried Crispy Meatballs.

Serves 7. Prep time: 20 minutes. Cooking: 15 minutes on high.
Suitable for: HP, KD, LC, LF, AK, WD.

Ingredients:
- 1.5 pounds low fat, grain-free ground sausage
- 1 egg, beaten

- 1 garlic clove, minced
- 1 teaspoon fresh parsley, minced
- Dash of salt and pepper
- ¼ cup breadcrumbs
- 1 kcal spray

Directions:
1. In a bowl, mix the ground sausage, egg, garlic, parsley, salt, pepper, and breadcrumbs. Roll into bite-size meatballs.
2. Spray meatballs with oil.
3. Place in air fryer. Cook at 350F for 15 minutes.

Nutritional values per serving: KCAL: 200; net C 7g; P 30g; F 9g.
Serve with gravy and a salad.

Air Fried Ham And Cheese Burgers.

Serves 5. Prep time: 10 minutes. Cooking: 10 minutes on medium.
Suitable for: HP, KD, LC, AK.

Ingredients:
- 1 cup ham, chopped
- ¾ cup sharp cheddar cheese
- 1 pound ground lean sausage
- 1 Tbsp Worcestershire sauce
- 1 Tbsp breadcrumbs
- salt and pepper to taste
- 1 kcal spray

Directions:
1. In a bowl, mix the chopped ham, cheese, sausage, Worcestershire sauce, breadcrumbs, salt, and pepper. Stir well. Shape into patties.
2. Shape into patties. Pat dry.
3. Spray both sides with oil.
4. Place in air fryer. Cook at 340F for 10 minutes.

Nutritional values per serving: KCAL: 150; net C 5g; P 31g; F 15g.
Serve on buns with a salad.

Air Fried Sausage Patties.

Serves 5. Prep time: 10 minutes. Cooking: 10 minutes on medium.
Suitable for: HP, KD, LC, AK, PL.

Ingredients:
- ½ cup fresh diced mushrooms
- 1 pound ground sausage
- 1 garlic clove, minced
- 1 tsp dried sage
- 1 tsp fresh or dried thyme
- 1 tsp dried fennel
- 1 Tbsp breadcrumbs
- salt and pepper to taste
- 1 kcal spray

Directions:
1. In a bowl, mix the mushrooms, sausage, garlic, sage, thyme, fennel, breadcrumbs, salt, and pepper. Mix well.
2. Shape into patties. Pat dry.
3. Spray both sides with oil.
4. Place patties in air fryer. Cook at 340F for 10 minutes.

Nutritional values per serving: KCAL: 134; net C 8g; P 28g; F 13g.
Serve on buns with a salad.

Air Fried Zucchini Loaf.

Serves 4. Prep time: 5 minutes. Cooking: 10 minutes on high.
Suitable for: LC, LF, VGI, VGN, PC.

Ingredients:
- 4 slices leftover zucchini bread
- 1 kcal spray
- ¼ cup flour
- salt and pepper to taste

Directions:
1. Spray both sides of load with oil. Season with salt and pepper.
2. Dip in flour.
3. Place in air fryer. Cook at 380F for 10 minutes.

Nutritional values per serving: *KCAL: net C 26g; P 8g; F 3g.*
Serve with steamed veggies.

Air Fried Cauliflower Cheese.

Serves 6. Prep time: 5 minutes. Cooking: 12 minutes on medium.
Suitable for: KD, LC, AK, VGI, PC, WD.

Ingredients:
- 1 head of cauliflower
- 2 cups béchamel sauce
- 1 cup grated cheese, mixed varieties
- salt and pepper to taste

Directions:
1. Peel off leaves. Rinse, and dry cauliflower. Chop into bite-size pieces.
2. In a bowl, mix the cauliflower, béchamel sauce, ½ cup of cheese, salt, and pepper. Stir well.
3. Spray 6 ramekins with oil.
4. Pour mixture into ramekins. Place in air fryer.

5. Cook at 325F for 12 minutes.
6. Add remaining cheese on top of cauliflower. Heat 1 – 2 minutes, until cheese melted.

Nutritional values per serving: KCAL: 230; net C 10g; P 16g; F 20g.
Serve with garlic bread.

Chapter 5: Desserts.

The range of delicious desserts that can be made using an air fryer is vast and amazing. This is because we aren't actually limited to the usual range of frying, but we can actually bake and steam foods in the air fryer. Which means that everything from brownies to doughnuts can be made quickly and healthily in our air fryer.

Air Fried Donuts.

Serves 4. Prep time: 10 minutes. Cooking: 20 minutes on high.
Suitable for: LF, VGI, PC.

Ingredients:
- 1 cup self-rising flour
- ½ cup sugar
- ½ cup whole milk
- 2.5 Tbsp butter, melted
- 1 egg
- Pinch of salt
- ¼ tsp pure vanilla extract
- 1 kcal spray
- Icing: powdered sugar with milk or cinnamon and sugar mix

Directions:
1. In a bowl, mix the melted butter and sugar. Add the flour slowly. Stir until slightly incorporated.
2. In a separate bowl, mix the milk and egg.
3. Add the flour to the liquid, slowly. Until it forms a ball and pulls away from the sides.
4. Dust the counter with flour. Knead the dough for 1 minute until it forms a smooth ball. Let it rest for 5 minutes.
5. Roll out the dough until 1 inch thick.
6. Use a medium size drinking glass, or a medium sized circle cutter to make your donuts.
7. Spray both sides of donuts with oil.
8. Place donuts in air fryer. Cook at 350F for 15 minutes.
9. Cool. Then dip in cinnamon and sugar or homemade icing.

Nutritional values per serving: KCAL: 230; net C 45g; P 3g; F 5g.
Serve as-is.

Air Fried Orange Chocolate Bites.

Serves 8. Prep time: 15 minutes. Cooking: 15 minutes on high.
Suitable for: LF, VGI, PC.

Ingredients:
- 1 cup self-rising flour
- ½ cup sugar
- ⅓ cup butter, room temperature
- juice from 1 orange
- 8 – 12 small cubes of dark chocolate
- 1 egg, beaten
- ¼ tsp vanilla
- pinch of salt
- oil

Directions:
1. In a bowl, mix the butter and flour until it forms crumbly mixture.
2. Mix in the sugar, vanilla, orange juice.
3. Add the egg. Stir until it forms a dough. If dough is still a bit wet, add more flour.
4. Pull off a pinch of dough, roll into bite-size ball.
5. Place on counter, flatten the ball. Place a piece of dark chocolate in middle. Roll the dough over chocolate piece.
6. Drizzle oil along bottom of air fryer. Place chocolate balls in air fryer.
7. Cook at 350F for 15 minutes.

Nutritional values per serving: KCAL: 230; net C 43g; P 8g; F 8g.
Serve dusted with sugar.

Air Fried Banana Bread.

Serves 8. Prep time: 10 minutes. Cooking: 35 minutes on low.
Suitable for: LF, VGI, PC, WD.

Ingredients:
- 1 cup self-rising flour
- 1 cup sugar
- 4 very ripe bananas
- 2 eggs
- 2 Tbsp butter
- 1 kcal spray

Directions:
1. Grease an air fryer cake or bread tin.
2. Cream the butter and sugar together.
3. Slowly add the eggs.
4. Mash the bananas and add to mixture.
5. Stir in flour, slowly.
6. Spray pan or tin with oil. Pour batter into pan or tin. Place in air fryer.
7. Cook at 400F for 35 minutes.

Nutritional values per serving: KCAL: 230; net C 46g; P 6g; F 7g.
Serve with butter.

Air Fried Oat Biscuit Sandwiches.

Serves 4. Prep time: 22 minutes. Cooking: 18 minutes on high.
Suitable for: LF, VGI, PC, WD.

Ingredients:
- 1 cup plain flour
- ⅓ cup butter, room temperature
- ½ cup shredded coconut
- ½ cup oats

- 1 beaten egg
- 3 Tbsp sugar
- 1 Tbsp pure vanilla extract
- oil
- 1 cup frosting

Directions:
1. Cream the butter and sugar together.
2. Add the egg, coconut, vanilla. Mix well.
3. Stir in the flour.
4. Roll into evenly sized balls and flatten into biscuits, ½ inch thick.
5. Drizzle oil over bottom of air fryer. Place in air fryer.
6. Cook at 380F for 18 minutes.
7. Cool completely.
8. Spread frosting between two cookies, press together.

Nutritional values per serving: *KCAL: 100; net C 20g; P 2g; F 3g.*
Serve as-is.

Air Fried Carrot Cake.

Serves 8. Prep time: 15 minutes. Cooking: 10 minutes on medium.
Suitable for: LF, VGI, PC, WD.

Ingredients:
- 1 cup self-rising flour
- 1 cup brown sugar
- 1.5 cups grated carrots
- 2 eggs, beaten
- juice from 1 orange
- 2 Tbsp mixed spices; cinnamon, nutmeg, ginger
- pinch of baking soda
- pinch of salt
- 1 kcal spray

Directions:

1. Spray air fryer cake/baking tin with oil.
2. In a bowl, mix the flour, carrots, baking soda, spices, and sugar. Stir well.
3. Add the eggs, orange juice. Stir.
4. Pour batter into cake/baking tin. Place in air fryer.
5. Cook at 380F for 5 minutes.
6. Reduce temperature to 325F. Cook for 5 more minutes.

Nutritional values per serving: KCAL: 130; net C 25g; P 4g; F 3g.
Serve with cream cheese icing.

Air Fried Lemon Bars.

Serves 8. Prep time: 5 minutes. Cooking: 5 minutes on high.
Suitable for: LC, LF, VGI, PC, WD.

Ingredients:
- 1 cup self-rising flour
- ⅔ cup sugar
- ⅓ cup melted butter
- Zest and juice from 1 lemon.
- 1 egg
- 1 tsp pure vanilla extract
- pinch of salt
- 1 kcal spray

Directions:
1. In a bowl, mix the dry ingredients.
2. Add melted butter until ingredients are a crumbly mixture.
3. Add lemon and egg. Stir well.
4. Mix until dough forms. Place dough on floured surface.
5. Cut into 2 inch by 2 inch long biscuits. Spray both sides of biscuits with oil.
6. Place on a baking sheet for air fryer. Place in air fryer.
7. Cook at 390F for 5 minutes.

Nutritional values per serving: KCAL: 55; net C 12g; P 1g; F 2g.
Serve dusted with icing sugar.

Air Fried Strawberry Cupcakes.

Serves 10. Prep time: 15 minutes. Cooking: 20 minutes on medium.
Suitable for: LC, VGI, PC.

Ingredients:
- 1 cup self-rising flour
- 1 cup sugar
- ⅓ cup butter, room temperature
- ⅓ cup strawberries, mashed
- 2 eggs
- ½ tsp pure vanilla extract
- strawberry or vanilla frosting
- sturdy cupcake liners
- 1 kcal spray

Directions:
1. Cream the butter and sugar together. Add the vanilla extract. Stir well.
2. Add the eggs. Mash the strawberries and add to batter.
3. Slowly fold in the flour.
4. Spray sturdy cupcake liners with oil. Fill liners ¾ full.
5. Place in air fryer. Cook at 340F for 20 minutes.
6. Cool before frosting.

Nutritional values per serving: *KCAL: 100; net C 20g; P 2g; F 11g.*
Serve with vanilla or strawberry frosting, or fresh strawberries.

Air Fried Cherry Lemon Cupcakes.

Serves 10. Prep time: 15 minutes. Cooking: 8 minutes on medium.
Suitable for: LC, VGI, PC.

Ingredients:
- 1 cup self-rising flour
- 1 cup sugar
- ⅓ cup butter, room temperature
- 2 eggs
- ½ tsp pure vanilla extract
- lemon juice and zest from 1 lemon
- 20 cherries, de-stemmed, pitted, minced
- lemon or cherry frosting
- 1 kcal spray

Directions:
1. Cream the butter and sugar together. Add vanilla extract. Stir well.
2. Add the eggs, diced cherries, lemon zest and lemon juice.
3. Fold in the flour. Stir until ingredients combined.
4. Spray sturdy cupcake liners with oil. Fill liners ¾ full.
5. Place in air fryer. Cook at 340F for 8 minutes.
6. Cool completely, then frost. Decorate with a cherry.

Nutritional values per serving: KCAL: 100; net C 18g; P 2g; F 12g.
Serve with icing; garnish with fresh cherry.

Air Fried Cookie Dough.

Serves 8. Prep time: 5 minutes. Cooking: 20 minutes on low.
Suitable for: LC, LF, VGI, PC, WD.

Ingredients:
- 1.5 cups self-rising flour
- ½ cup sugar

- ⅓ cup butter, room temperature
- ⅓ cup chocolate
- ¼ tsp pure vanilla extract
- 1 Tbsp milk
- 1 kcal spray

Directions:
1. Cream the butter and sugar together. Add the vanilla.
2. Smash your chocolate into chips and stir in.
3. Fold in flour. Stir in milk.
4. Spray appropriate baking tin with oil. Place in air fryer.
5. Cook at 325F for 20 minutes.

Nutritional values per serving: KCAL: net C 34g; P 1g; F 9g.
Serve warm, with ice cream.

Air Fried Pineapple Cake.

Serves 4. Prep time: 10 minutes. Cooking: 40 minutes on medium.
Suitable for: LC, LF, VGI, VGN, PC.

Ingredients:
- 1 cup self-rising flour
- ⅓ cup sugar
- ⅓ cup margarine, softened
- 1 tin pineapple rings in juice
- 3 Tbsp applesauce
- 1 kcal spray

Directions:
1. Mix the margarine and flour into a crumble.
2. Add the sugar and pineapple juice. Mix well.
3. Add the applesauce. Stir until the batter is smooth.
4. Spray air fryer cake tin with oil. Layer pineapple rings along the bottom. Pour in the batter. Place in air fryer.

5. Cook at 325F for 40 minutes. Cool for 10 minutes before turning out of tin.

Nutritional values per serving: KCAL: 130; net C 37g; P 4g; F 8g.
Serve with whipped cream.

Air Fried Sponge Cake.

Serves 8. Prep time: 15 minutes. Cooking: 30 minutes on high.
Suitable for: LC, VGI, PC.

Ingredients:
- 1 cup plain flour
- ⅓ cup butter, room temperature
- ⅓ cup sugar
- ¼ tsp pure vanilla extract
- 2 eggs
- strawberry jam
- cream
- 1 kcal spray

Directions:
1. Spray air fryer baking dish with kcal oil.
2. Cream the butter and the sugar together. Add the vanilla.
3. Add the eggs. Stir well.
4. Slowly fold in the flour.
5. Pour into greased dish. Place in air fryer.
6. Cook at 350F for 15 minutes.
7. Reduce temperature to 340F, cook for 15 more minutes.
8. Cool completely. Layer with jam and cream, dust with icing sugar.

Nutritional values per serving: KCAL: 200; net C 36g; P 6g; F 19g.
Serve dusted with icing sugar, side of fresh fruit.

Air Fried Chocolate Brownies.

Serves 4. Prep time: 15 minutes. Cooking: 40 minutes on high.
Suitable for: LC, VGI, PC, WD.

Ingredients:
- 1 cup self-rising flour
- 2 cups sugar
- 1 egg
- ½ cup milk
- ½ cup butter
- ¼ cup chocolate
- 1 tsp pure vanilla extract
- 1 kcal spray

Directions:
1. Melt the butter and chocolate together.
2. Whisk the egg and sugar together.
3. Combine butter mixture with egg mixture by adding a small amount of warm chocolate mixture to the egg slowly; this is tempering - allows the egg to adjust to temperature and doesn't cook the egg. Stir in rest of chocolate.
4. Add the vanilla extract and milk.
5. Fold in the flour.
6. Pour into a greased air fryer baking tray. Place in air fryer.
7. Cook at 350F for 40 minutes.
8. Serve warm.

Nutritional values per serving: KCAL: 210; net C 36g; P 11g; F 15g.
Serve with ice cream.

Air Fried New York Cheesecake.

Serves 8. Prep time: 20 minutes. Cooking: 45 minutes on high.
Suitable for: LC, AK, VGI, PC, WD.

Ingredients:
- 1.5 cups flour
- 3 cups sugar
- ⅓ cup butter, melted
- 2 x 8 ounce packages cream cheese, room temperature
- 3 eggs, room temperature
- 1 tsp pure vanilla extract
- 1 kcal spray

Directions:
1. Mix the flour and a cup of sugar. Add the butter in to create a crumb.
2. Line air fryer cake pan with parchment paper. Spray with oil. Press the crumb mixture in an even layer along bottom of tin.
3. Cook at 350F for 15 minutes.
4. Beat the cream cheese to smooth consistency (1 – 2 minutes).
5. Add remaining 2 cups of sugar. Beat until combined.
6. Add the eggs one at a time, beat until combined.
7. Add the vanilla. Beat for 1 minute.
8. Pour over top of baked crust. Place in air fryer.
9. Cook at 350F for 30 minutes.
10. Cool before slicing.

Nutritional values per serving: KCAL: 230; net C 19g; P 9g; F 18g.
Serve with a dusting of cocoa, whip cream.

Air Fried Chocolate Chip Cookies.

Serves 8. Prep time: 5 minutes. Cooking: 10 minutes on medium.
Suitable for: LC, LF, VGI, PC, WD.

Ingredients:
- 1 cup self-rising flour
- ⅓ cup butter, room temperature
- ⅓ cup chocolate chips
- ⅓ cup sugar
- 1 Tbsp milk
- 1 tsp cinnamon
- 1 kcal spray

Directions:
1. In a bowl, mix the sugar and butter.
2. Add the flour, cinnamon, chocolate chips. Stir.
3. Add the milk. Stir until the batter forms a ball.
4. Pinch off pieces of batter. Roll into bite-size balls.
5. Line air fryer basket with parchment paper. Spray dough balls with oil. (Arrange dough balls in basket, making sure they don't touch.)
6. Cook at 340F for 10 minutes.

Nutritional values per serving: *KCAL: 100; net C 20g; P 2g; F 7g.*
Serve with a glass of milk.

Air Fried Lime Cheesecake.

Serves 8. Prep time: 20 minutes. Cooking: 45 minutes on high.
Suitable for: LC, AK, VGI, PC, WD.

Ingredients:
- 1 cup flour
- 3 cups sugar
- ⅓ cup butter, melted
- 2 x 8 ounce packages of cream cheese, softened
- Juice and zest from 2 limes
- 3 eggs
- 1 Tbsp pure vanilla extract
- 1 kcal spray

Directions:
1. Mix the flour and 1 cup of the sugar. Add the melted butter to create a crumb.
2. Line air fryer cake tin with parchment paper. Press crumb mix in an even layer along bottom of cake tin. Spray with kcal oil.
3. Cook at 350F for 15 minutes. Remove and set aside. Allow to cool slightly before adding cheesecake batter.
4. Beat the cream cheese to smooth consistency (1 – 2 minutes).
5. Add the sugar. Beat until smooth.
6. Add eggs one at a time, beat until incorporated.
7. Add the lime juice and zest. Stir until smooth.
8. Pour over top of baked crust. Place in air fryer.
9. Cook at 350F for 30 minutes.
10. Cool before slicing.

Nutritional values per serving: KCAL: 230; net C 19g; P 9g; F 18g.
Serve with a sprinkle of lime zest, whipped cream.

Chapter 6: Snacks.

I'm not sure about you, but when I think about snack foods I think of a deep, satisfying crunch. So it can be hard to start trying to eat healthy, when the snacks we love are so delicious and crispy, and fruits and veggies are so... not. But there is a way around this using the air fryer! We can make delightful and crispy, healthy snacks at home using our air fryer. Veggie chips anyone?

Air Fried Zucchini Fries.

Serves 3. Prep time: 10 minutes. Cooking: 20 minutes on high.
Suitable for: LC, LF, VGI, PC, WD.

Ingredients:
- 1 pound zucchini
- 2 large egg whites
- ½ cup flour with garlic and onion powder
- ½ cup breadcrumbs
- 1 tsp garlic powder
- 1 tsp parmesan cheese
- 1 kcal spray
- salt and pepper

Directions:
1. Cut zucchini into sticks. Pat dry.
2. Beat egg whites with salt and pepper.
3. Dip your sticks into flour, then eggs, then breadcrumbs. Repeat for a crunchier coating.
4. Spray battered zucchini with oil. Place in air fryer.
5. Cook at 350F for 20 minutes.

Nutritional values per serving: KCAL: 80; net C 12g; P 3g; F 4g.
Serve with a ranch sauce for dipping, or as a side dish.

Air Fried Pickles.

Serves 3. Prep time: 10 minutes. Cooking: 20 minutes on high.
Suitable for: KD, LC, LF, VGI, PC, WD.

Ingredients:
- 1 pound dill pickles, sliced
- 2 large egg whites
- ½ cup flour
- 1 tsp onion powder
- ½ cup breadcrumbs
- 1 tsp dried dill leaves
- 1 kcal spray
- salt and pepper

Directions:
1. Slice dill pickles. Pat dry.
2. Beat egg whites with salt and pepper.
3. Dip pickle slices in flour, then eggs, then breadcrumbs. Repeat for crunchier crust.
4. Spray them with oil. Place in air fryer.
5. Cook at 340F for 20 minutes.

Nutritional values per serving: KCAL: 50; net C 6g; P 3g; F 4g.
Serve with ranch sauce for dipping, or as a side dish.

Air Fried Seafood Snacks.

Serves 4. Prep time: 5 minutes. Cooking: 12 minutes on medium.
Suitable for: HP, KD, LC, LF, AK, PC.

Ingredients:
- 16 crab sticks
- 1 Tbsp sesame seed oil
- sea salt

Directions:
1. Unroll the crab sticks. Pat dry. Tear them into strips.
2. Toss with the sesame seed oil.
3. Place in air fry. Cook at 325F for 12 minutes.
4. Season cooked crab with sea salt.

Nutritional values per serving: KCAL: 120; net C 7g; P 22g; F 3g.
Serve as-is.

Air Fried Butternut Squash Fries.

Serves 3. Prep time: 10 minutes. Cooking: 20 minutes on high.
Suitable for: LC, LF, VGI, PC, WD.

Ingredients:
- 1 pound butternut squash
- 2 large egg whites
- ½ cup flour
- 1 tsp onion powder
- ½ cup breadcrumbs
- 1 kcal spray
- salt and pepper

Directions:
1. Peel the squash and remove the seeds.
2. Cut into sticks. Pat dry.
3. Beat egg whites with salt and pepper.
4. Dip sticks into flour, then eggs, then breadcrumbs. Repeat for crunchier crust.
5. Spray the battered sticks with oil. Place in air fryer.
6. Cook at 350F for 20 minutes.

Nutritional values per serving: KCAL: 110; net C 12g; P 3g; F 4g.
Serve with sauce for dipping, or as a side dish.

Air Fried Kale Chips.

Serves 5. Prep time: 1 minute. Cooking: 2 minutes on high.
Suitable for: KD, LC, LF, AK, PL, VGI, VGN, PC, WD.

Ingredients:
- 1 medium head of kale
- 1 Tbsp sesame seed, coconut, or olive oil
- 1 tsp onion powder
- 1 tsp salt and pepper

Directions:
1. Remove centre stem of kale. Rinse leaves and pat dry.
2. Tear or chop into even-ish squares.
3. Toss the leaves with oil. Season with onion powder. Place in air fryer.
4. Fry at 400F for 2 minutes.
5. Season with salt and pepper.

Nutritional values per serving: KCAL: 13; net C 2g; P 0g; F 1g.
Serve with a dip, or as a side dish.

Air Fried Salmon Croquettes.

Serves 4. Prep time: 10 minutes. Cooking: 7 minutes on high.
Suitable for: LC, PC, WD.

Ingredients:
- 1 pound red salmon, cooked or from a tin
- ⅓ cup breadcrumbs
- 1 tsp onion powder
- ½ tsp fresh parsley
- ½ tsp fresh dill
- 2 eggs
- ⅓ cup oil
- herbes du provence

Directions:

1. In a large bowl, combine the salmon, egg, herbes, parsley, and dill. Mix well.
2. Roll into bite-size balls.
3. Spray the salmon balls with oil. Roll in breadcrumbs. Spray with oil again.
4. Place in air fryer.
5. Cook at 400F for 7 minutes. In small batches, so they don't stick.

Nutritional values per serving: *KCAL: 230; net C 32g; P 11g; F 17g.*
Serve with dipping sauce.

Air Fried Cayenne Carrot Fries.

Serves 3. Prep time: 10 minutes. Cooking: 20 minutes on high.
Suitable for: LC, LF, VGI, PC, WD.

Ingredients:

- 1 pound carrots, peeled
- 2 large egg whites
- ½ cup flour
- 1 tsp cayenne pepper
- ½ tsp garlic powder
- ½ tsp onion powder
- ½ cup breadcrumbs
- 1 tsp chili flakes
- 1 kcal spray
- salt and pepper

Directions:

1. Cut carrots into sticks. Pat dry.
2. Beat egg whites with salt and pepper.
3. Season breadcrumbs with cayenne pepper, garlic powder, onion powder, chili flakes.
4. Dip carrot sticks in flour, then eggs, then breadcrumbs. Repeat for crunchier coating.

5. Spray battered carrots with oil. Place in air fryer.
6. Cook at 350F for 20 minutes.

Nutritional values per serving: KCAL: 80; net C 7g; P 3g; F 4g.
Serve with sauce for dipping, or as a side dish.

Air Fried Red Cabbage Chips.

Serves 5. Prep time: 1 minute. Cooking: 2 minutes on high.
Suitable for: KD, LC, LF, AK, PL, VGI, VGN, PC, WD.

Ingredients:
- 1 medium head of red cabbage
- 1 Tbsp sesame seed, coconut, or olive oil
- 1 tsp brown sugar

Directions:
1. Remove centre stem of cabbage. Rinse leaves and pat dry.
2. Tear or chop into even-ish squares.
3. Toss leaves in oil. Place in air fryer.
4. Cook at 400F for 2 minutes.
5. Toss the chips with brown sugar.

Nutritional values per serving: KCAL: 29; net C 5g; P 0g; F 1g.
Serve with a dip, or as a side dish.

Air Fried Honey Lime Chicken Wings.

Serves 4. Prep time: 15 minutes. Cooking: 10 minutes on high.
Suitable for: HP, LC, LF, AK, WD.

Ingredients:
- 16 chicken wings

- ½ cup rice flour
- ¼ cup water
- 2 Tbsp honey
- 2 Tbsp lime juice
- 1 Tbsp soy sauce
- salt and pepper
- oil

Directions:
1. Rinse wings and pat dry.
2. In a baggie, combine the water, honey, lime, soy sauce, salt, and pepper. Massage the marinade into the wings to coat evenly. Marinate the wings in fridge from 20 minutes to 2 hours.
3. Take wings out of marinade. Dip the wings in flour. Place in air fryer.
4. Cook at 400F for 10 minutes.

Nutritional values per serving: *KCAL: 170; net C 12g; P 20g; F 4g.*
Serve with a dip or fries.

Air Fried Parmesan Romaine Chips.

Serves 5. Prep time: 1 minute. Cooking: 2 minutes on high.
Suitable for: KD, LC, LF, AK, PL, VGI, VGN, PC, WD.

Ingredients:
- 1 medium head of romaine
- 1 Tbsp sesame seed, coconut, or olive oil
- salt and pepper

Directions:
1. Remove centre stem of romaine. Rinse leaves and pat dry.
2. Tear or chop into even-ish squares.
3. Toss leaves in oil. Place in air fryer.
4. Cook at 400F for 2 minutes.
5. Season with salt and pepper.

Nutritional values per serving: KCAL: 17; net C 2g; P 0g; F 1g.
Serve with a dip, or as a side dish.

Air Fried Parsnip Fries.

Serves 3. Prep time: 10 minutes. Cooking: 20 minutes on high.
Suitable for: LC, LF, VGI, VGN, PC.

Ingredients:
- 1 pound parsnips, peeled
- 2 eggs
- ½ cup flour
- 1 tsp fresh or dried rosemary
- 1 tsp garlic powder
- ½ cup breadcrumbs
- 1 kcal spray
- salt and pepper

Directions:
1. Cut parsnips into sticks. Pat dry.
2. Season breadcrumbs with rosemary, salt, and pepper.
3. Dip sticks into flour, then egg, then breadcrumbs. Repeat for crunchier coating.
4. Spray with oil. Place in air fryer.
5. Cook at 350F for 20 minutes.

Nutritional values per serving: KCAL: 130; net C 17g; P 3g; F 7g.
Serve with sauce for dipping, or as a side dish.

Air Fried Cheese and Ham Croquettes.

Serves 4. Prep time: 10 minutes. Cooking: 7 minutes on high.
Suitable for: LC, PL, WD.

Ingredients:
- ½ pound boiled ham, chopped
- ½ pound sharp cheddar cheese, chopped
- ⅓ cup potato, cooked and mashed
- 2 eggs, beaten
- ½ cup flour
- 1 cup breadcrumbs
- ⅓ cup oil

Directions:
1. Mash the potatoes. In a separate bowl, combine the ham and cheese.
2. Roll potatoes into bite-size balls.
3. Press your thumb into middle of mashed potatoe ball, fill with ham and cheese mixture. Roll closed.
4. Roll balls in flour, then egg mixture, then breadcrumbs.
5. Drizzle oil in air fryer. Place croquettes in air fryer.
6. Cook at 400F for 7 minutes. In small batches, so they don't stick.

Nutritional values per serving: KCAL: 300; net C 36g; P 19g; F 20g.
Serve with dipping sauce.

Air Fried Buffalo Wings.

Serves 4. Prep time: 15 minutes. Cooking: 10 minutes on high.
Suitable for: HP, KD, LC, LF, AK.

Ingredients:
- 16 chicken wing
- ½ cup rice flour
- buffalo sauce

- oil

Directions:

1. Rinse wings and pat dry.
2. Pour the buffalo sauce in a large plastic baggie. Drop the wings in the bag. Massage to coat evenly. Marinade in fridge 20 minutes to 2 hours.
3. Remove wings from marinade. Dip in flour.
4. Drizzle oil along bottom of air fryer. Place wings in air fryer.
5. Cook at 400F for 10 minutes.

Nutritional values per serving: KCAL: 130; net C 7g; P 20g; F 4g.
Serve with a dip or fries.

Air Fried Toasted Chickpeas.

Serves 3. Prep time: 2 minutes. Cooking: 10 minutes on high.
Suitable for: LC, LF, VGI, VGN, PC, WD.

Ingredients:

- 1 can of chickpeas, drained
- 1 Tbsp Mexican spice mix
- oil

Directions:

1. Toss chickpeas until dry. Add spices and toss some more.
2. Drizzle oil along bottom of air fryer. Place chicken peas in air fryer, careful they don't touch.
3. Cook at 350F for 10 minutes.

Nutritional values per serving: KCAL: 100; net C 20g; P 3g; F 2g.
Serve as-is.

Air Fried Crunchy Potato Chips.

Serves 2. Prep time: 5 minutes. Cooking: 20 minutes on high.
Suitable for: LF, PL, VGI, VGN, PC, WD.

Ingredients:
- 2 potatoes, washed (peeled or unpeeled)
- 1 Tbsp olive oil
- Salt

Directions:
1. Using a mandolin slice the potatoes thinly.
2. Rinse the slices in cold water a few times, and pat dry.
3. Toss with oil. Place in air fryer, careful they don't touch.
4. Air fry at 400F for 20 minutes. Season with salt once cooked.

Nutritional values per serving: *KCAL: 110; net C 20g; P 2g; F 2g.*
Serve as-is.

Chapter 7: Proteins

Protein sources are often overlooked when it comes to air frying. But really, there are countless amazing ways of cooking proteins in an air fryer, if only you know how. Many of these recipes focus on traditionally deep fried foods, such as wings and croquettes, to give them a new, healthy twist. Which means you can enjoy your usual junk-food-tasting favourites, guilt free!

Air Fried Chinese Style Wings.

Serves 2. Prep time: 15 minutes. Cooking: 10 minutes on high.
Suitable for: HP, LF.

Ingredients:
- 16 chicken wings
- ½ cup rice flour
- 1 Tbsp brown sugar
- 1 Tbsp garlic powder
- soy sauce
- oil

Directions:
1. Rinse the wings, pat dry.
2. In a small saucepan, heat soy sauce, brown sugar, and garlic. Set aside to cool.
3. In a large baggie, combine the soy sauce mixture and the wings. Massage until evenly coated. Marinade in fridge for 20 minutes up to 2 hours.
4. Remove the wings from marinade, dip in flour.
5. Drizzle oil over bottom of air fryer. Place wings in air fryer.
6. Cook at 400F for 10 minutes.

Nutritional values per serving: KCAL: 410; net C 52g; P 40g; F 8g.
Serve with sweet and sour sauce.

Air Fried Cajun Salmon.

Serves 1. Prep time: 10 minutes. Cooking: 7 minutes on medium.
Suitable for: HP, KD, LC, LF, AK, PL, PC, WD.

Ingredients:
- 1 x 7 ounce fillet of salmon
- 1 Tbsp cajun seasoning
- oil

Directions:
1. Rub cajun seasoning into the salmon.
2. Drizzle oil along bottom of air fryer. Place salmon in air fryer.
3. Cook at 350F for 7 minutes.

Nutritional values per serving: KCAL: 210; net C 4g; P 43g; F 9g.
Serve with a salad and/or rice and steamed vegetables.

Air Fried Coconut Chicken.

Serves 4. Prep time: 10 minutes. Cooking: 12 minutes on high.
Suitable for: HP, LC, AK, WD.

Ingredients:
- 1 pound chicken breasts, sliced into strips
- ½ cup flour
- ¾ cup shredded coconut
- ¾ cup breadcrumbs
- 2 eggs, beaten
- 1 tsp paprika
- 1 kcal spray
- salt and pepper
- oil

Directions:

1. Rinse the chicken, slice into strips. Pat dry.
2. Season the flour with paprika, salt, and pepper.
3. Combine the breadcrumbs and coconut.
4. Dip the chicken in flour, then egg mixture, then breadcrumbs.
5. Drizzle oil along bottom of air fryer. Place chicken in air fryer.
6. Cook at 400F for 12 minutes.

Nutritional values per serving: KCAL: 190; net C 14g; P 24g; F 14g.
Serve with dips and a side salad.

Air Fried Crunchy Wings.

Serves 4. Prep time: 15 minutes. Cooking: 10 minutes on high.
Suitable for: LC, LF.

Ingredients:
- 16 chicken wings
- 2 eggs
- ½ cup flour
- 1 tsp garlic powder
- 1 tsp onion powder
- Salt and pepper to taste
- ½ cup breadcrumbs
- oil

Directions:
1. Rinse the wings, pat them dry.
2. Mix the breadcrumbs with the garlic powder, onion powder, salt, and pepper. Dip the wings in flour, then eggs, then breadcrumbs.
3. Repeat; dip in flour, eggs, then breadcrumbs.
4. Drizzle oil along bottom of air fryer. Place wings in air fryer.
5. Cook at 400F for 10 minutes.

Nutritional values per serving: KCAL: 180; net C 30g; P 18g; F 5g.
Serve with a dip or fries.

Air Fried Lemon Sole.

Serves 1. Prep time: 10 minutes. Cooking: 7 minutes on medium.
Suitable for: HP, KD, LC, LF, AK, PL, PC, WD.

Ingredients:
- 1 x 6 ounce fillet of sole
- lemon juice
- salt and pepper
- oil

Directions:
1. Rinse the fillet. Drizzle lemon juice over the fillet. Season with salt and pepper.
2. Drizzle oil along bottom of air fryer. Place sole in air fryer.
3. Cook at 350F for 7 minutes.

Nutritional values per serving: KCAL: 190; net C 4g; P 36g; F 9g.
Serve with a salad and/or rice and steamed vegetables.

Air Fried Smoked Haddock Croquettes.

Serves 4. Prep time: 10 minutes. Cooking: 7 minutes on high.
Suitable for: HP, PC, WD.

Ingredients:
- 1 pound smoked haddock, minced
- ⅓ cup mashed potato
- 2 -3 Tbsp butter/margarine
- 1 – 2 Tbsp milk
- ½ cup flour
- ½ cup breadcrumbs
- 2 eggs, beaten
- Salt and pepper to taste
- ⅓ cup oil

Directions:

1. Season the flour with salt and pepper.
2. Mash the potatoes. Add butter and milk. Stir until smooth.
3. Roll into bite-size balls.
4. Break up the cooked haddock. Press a thumb-size into middle of potatoe ball. Fill with haddock mixture. Roll closed.
5. Roll in flour, then egg, then breadcrumbs.
6. Drizzle oil along bottom of air fryer. Place croquettes in air fryer.
7. Cook at 400F for 7 minutes. In small batches, so they don't stick.

Nutritional values per serving: *KCAL: 320; net C 43g; P 22g; F 13g.*
Serve with dipping sauce.

Air Fried Teriyaki Wings.

Serves 2. Prep time: 15 minutes. Cooking: 10 minutes on high.
Suitable for: HP, LC, LF, AK.

Ingredients:

- 16 chicken wings
- ½ cup rice flour
- teriyaki sauce
- oil

Directions:

1. Rinse and pat wings dry.
2. Pour teriyaki sauce in a large baggie. Place wings in baggie with sauce. Massage until wings are coated. Marinate in fridge from 20 minutes up to 2 hours.
3. Drizzle oil over bottom of air fryer. Dip the wings in rice flour. Place in air fryer.
4. Cook at 400F for 10 minutes.

Nutritional values per serving: *KCAL: 320; net C 24g; P 40g; F 10g.*
Serve with salad and fries.

Air Fried Lamb Steak.

Serves 1. Prep time: 10 minutes. Cooking: 7 minutes on medium.
Suitable for: HP, KD, LC, LF, AK, PL, WD.

Ingredients:
- 1 x 6 ounce lamb steak
- 1 tsp finely minced mint
- 1 tsp garlic powder
- Pinch of salt
- oil

Directions:
1. Mix mint, garlic powder, and salt in a bowl. Rub the seasoning into lamb.
2. Drizzle oil over bottom of air fryer. Place lamb steak in air fryer.
3. Cook at 350F for 7 minutes.

Nutritional values per serving: KCAL: 200; net C 3g; P 30g; F 12g.
Serve with a salad and/or rice and steamed vegetables.

Air Fried Turkey and Cranberry Croquettes.

Serves 4. Prep time: 10 minutes. Cooking: 7 minutes on high.
Suitable for: HP, LC, LF.

Ingredients:
- 1 pound lean ground turkey
- ⅓ cup breadcrumbs or stuffing mix
- 4 Tbsp cranberry sauce
- 2 eggs, beaten
- ½ cup flour
- oil

Directions:
1. In a bowl combine the ground turkey, cranberry sauce.

2. Roll into bite-size pieces.
3. Dip the pieces in flour, then egg, then breadcrumbs.
4. Drizzle oil along bottom of air fryer.
5. Place croquettes in air fryer.
6. Cook at 400F for 7 minutes. In small batches, so they don't stick.

Nutritional values per serving: KCAL: 210; net C 32g; P 24g; F 6g.
Serve with dipping sauce.

Air Fried Breaded Beef.

Serves 4. Prep time: 10 minutes. Cooking: 12 minutes on high.
Suitable for: HP, LC, LF, AK, WD.

Ingredients:
- 1 pound beef steak, sliced into bite-size pieces
- ½ cup flour
- 1 cup breadcrumbs
- 2 eggs, beaten
- steak seasoning
- 1 kcal spray
- salt and pepper
- oil

Directions:
1. Mix the eggs and half the steak seasoning.
2. Mix the breadcrumbs and remaining steak seasoning.
3. Dip the beef in the flour, then eggs, then the breadcrumbs.
4. Drizzle oil along bottom of air fryer. Place pieces in air fryer.
5. Cook at 400F for 12 minutes.

Nutritional values per serving: KCAL: 190; net C 21g; P 24g; F 6g.
Serve with dip and salad.

Air Fried Sweet and Sour Wings.

Serves 4. Prep time: 15 minutes. Cooking: 10 minutes on high.
Suitable for: HP, LC, AK.

Ingredients:
- 16 chicken wings
- 1 cup sweet and sour sauce
- ½ cup rice flour
- oil

Directions:
1. Rinse wings and pat dry.
2. In a large baggie, pour in sweet and sour sauce. Add the wings. Massage until wings are evenly coated. Marinate in fridge from 20 minutes up to 2 hours.
3. Dip the wings in flour.
4. Drizzle oil over bottom of air fryer. Place wings in air fryer.
5. Cook at 400F for 10 minutes.

Nutritional values per serving: KCAL: 207; net C 34g; P 20g; F 17g.
Serve with salad.

Air Fried Spicy Curry Wings.

Serves 4. Prep time: 15 minutes. Cooking: 10 minutes on high.
Suitable for: HP, LC, AK, WD.

Ingredients:
- 16 chicken wings
- 1 tsp curry powder
- 1 tsp coriander powder
- 1 tsp cumin powder
- ½ cup coconut milk
- ½ cup rice flour
- oil

Directions:

1. Rinse wings and pat dry.
2. In a large baggie, combine coconut milk and spices. Add the wings. Massage until wings are coated. Marinate in fridge from 20 minutes up to 2 hours.
3. After marinating, dip wings in flour.
4. Drizzle oil over bottom of air fryer. Place wings in air fryer.
5. Cook wings at 400F for 10 minutes. After 10 minutes, you could turn the wings, cook for another 5 minutes.

Nutritional values per serving: KCAL: 214; net C 12g; P 20g; F 17g.
Serve with rice.

Air Fried Kippers.

Serves 1. Prep time: 10 minutes. Cooking: 7 minutes on medium.
Suitable for: HP, KD, LC, AK, PL, PC.

Ingredients:

- 1 x 7 ounces kipper
- 1 tsp butter

Directions:

1. Rub the butter into your kipper. Fan it out in the basket.
2. Place in air fryer.
3. Cook at 350F for 7 minutes. Best served immediately.

Nutritional values per serving: KCAL: 210; net C 4g; P 35g; F 13g.
Serve with eggs.

Air Fried Spicy Crunchy Prawns.

Serves 4. Prep time: 10 minutes. Cooking: 7 minutes on high.
Suitable for: HP, LC, LF, AK, WD.

Ingredients:
- 1 pound cooked prawns, shelled
- 1 cup breadcrumbs
- ½ cup flour
- 2 eggs, beaten
- 1 tsp chili flakes
- 1 kcal spray
- salt and pepper
- oil

Directions:
1. Rinse the prawns and pat dry.
2. Mix eggs with salt and pepper. Mix the breadcrumbs and chili flakes.
3. Dip the prawns in the flour, then eggs, then the breadcrumbs. Repeat for crunchier coating.
4. Spray the coated prawns with oil. Place in air fryer.
5. Cook at 400F for 7 minutes.

Nutritional values per serving: KCAL: 120; net C 14g; P 24g; F 2g.
Serve with dip and side salad.

Air Fried Battered King Prawns.

Serves 4. Prep time: 10 minutes. Cooking: 7 minutes on high.
Suitable for: HP, LC, LF, AK, WD.

Ingredients:
- 1 pound cooked prawns, shelled
- 1 cup batter (1 cup flour, 1 egg, ½ beer)
- 1 tsp garlic powder

- 1 tsp onion powder
- 1 tsp chili flakes
- 1 tsp salt
- 1 tsp pepper
- 1 kcal spray

Directions:
1. Mix the batter.
2. Rinse the prawns and pat dry.
3. Dip the prawns in batter. Seal in boiling water immediately; to create a dumpling texture.
4. Drizzle oil along bottom of air fryer. Place prawns in air fryer.
5. Cook at 400F for 7 minutes.

Nutritional values per serving: *KCAL: 120; net C 22g; P 24g; F 2g.*
Serve with dip and side salad.

Chapter 8: Starches

Starches are a quintessential air fryer food. This is because on almost every diet a starch can be our downfall, due to the usual high oil, salty, moorish qualities they have, and also because air frying dries out starchy foods, giving them that amazing crunch we want!

Air Fried French Fries.

Serves 4. Prep time: 5 minutes. Cooking: 9 minutes on medium.
Suitable for: LC, LF, VGI, VGN, PC.

Ingredients:
- 1 pound starchy potatoes
- 1.5 Tbsp sunflower oil
- salt

Directions:
1. Peel your potatoes and slice them thinly.
2. Rinse in cold water a few times until water runs clear.
3. Coat the potatoes in oil. Place potatoes in air fryer.
4. Cook at 350F for 9 minutes.
5. Season with salt.

Nutritional values per serving: KCAL: 120; net C 25g; P 2g; F 3g.
Serve as a side dish.

Air Fried Curly Fries.

Serves 4. Prep time: 5 minutes. Cooking: 9 minutes on medium.
Suitable for: LC, LF, VGI, VGN, PC.

Ingredients:
- 1 pound starchy potatoes
- 1.5 Tbsp sunflower oil
- salt

Directions:
1. Peel the potatoes. Using a spiralizer, create curly fires.
2. Rinse in cold water until water runs clear.
3. Slide potatoes on skewers to maintain curly shape.
4. Coat the potatoes in oil. (It is easier to coat them in oil once on the skewers.) Place potatoes in air fryer.
5. Cook at 350F for 9 minutes.
6. Season with salt.

Nutritional values per serving: KCAL: 120; net C 25g; P 2g; F 3g.
Serve as a side dish.

Air Fried Sweet Potato Fries.

Serves 4. Prep time: 5 minutes. Cooking: 9 minutes on medium.
Suitable for: LC, LF, PL, VGI, VGN, PC.

Ingredients:
- 1 pound sweet potatoes
- 1.5 Tbsp coconut oil
- salt

Directions:
1. Peel the potatoes. Slice into sticks. Rinse in cold water.
2. Coat the potatoes in oil. Place potatoes in air fryer.
3. Cook at 350F for 9 minutes.
4. Season with salt.

Nutritional values per serving: KCAL: 130; net C 27g; P 2g; F 3g.
Serve as a side dish,

Air Fried English Chip Shop Fries.

Serves 4. Prep time: 5 minutes. Cooking: 12 minutes on medium.
Suitable for: LC, LF, VGI, VGN, PC.

Ingredients:
- 1 pound starchy potatoes
- 1.5 Tbsp sunflower oil
- salt
- malt vinegar

Directions:
1. Peel the potatoes. Slice them into thick fingers.
2. Rinse in cold water until water runs clear. Coat potatoes in oil. Place in air fryer.
3. Cook at 350F for 12 minutes.
4. Season with salt, sprinkle with vinegar.

Nutritional values per serving: KCAL: 120; net C 25g; P 2g; F 3g.
Serve as a side dish.

Air Fried Yam Fries.

Serves 4. Prep time: 5 minutes. Cooking: 9 minutes on medium.
Suitable for: LC, LF, VGI, VGN, PC.

Ingredients:
- 1 pound yams
- 1.5 Tbsp sesame seed oil
- salt

Directions:
1. Peel the yams. Slice into circles.
2. Rinse in cold water. Coat the yam slices in oil. Place in air fryer.
3. Cook at 325F for 9 minutes.
4. Season with salt.

Nutritional values per serving: KCAL: 80; net C 18g; P 2g; F 3g.
Serve as a side dish.

Air Fried 3 Flavors of Chips.

Serves 2. Prep time: 5 minutes. Cooking: 20 minutes on high.
Suitable for: LF, LC, PL, VGI, VGN, PC, WD.

Ingredients:
- ½ pound potatoes
- ½ Tbsp olive oil
- Mix 1: onion powder, garlic powder, nutritional yeast
- Mix 2: smoked paprika, black pepper, coriander
- Mix 3: bacon salt, sugar, black pepper

Directions:
1. Using a mandolin, slice the potatoes to ¼ inch thickness.
2. Rinse in cold water until the water runs clear.
3. Coat with oil. Place in air fryer.
4. Cook at 400F for 20 minutes.
5. Toss each batch in one of the mixes.

Nutritional values per serving: KCAL: 110; net C 20g; P 2g; F 2g.
Serve as-is.

Air Fried Mashed Potatoe Croquettes.

Serves 4. Prep time: 5 minutes. Cooking: 5 minutes on high.
Suitable for: LC, LF, VGI, VGN, PC.

Ingredients:
- 1 pound mashed potatoes
- 2 – 3 Tbsp butter
- 1 – 2 Tbsp milk
- ½ cup flour
- 1 egg, beaten
- ½ cup breadcrumbs
- 1 kcal spray

- Pinch of salt, pepper, cayenne pepper

Directions:
1. Mash the potatoes.
2. Add salt, pepper, cayenne better, butter, and milk. Mash until smooth.
3. Pinch off bite-size amount of mashed potatoes. Roll into bite-size piece.
4. Roll in flour, then egg, then breadcrumbs.
5. Spray with oil. Place in air fryer.
6. Cook at 325F for 9 minutes.

Nutritional values per serving: KCAL: 115; net C 27g; P 2g; F 1g.
Serve as a side dish.

Air Fried Taro Chips.

Serves 2. Prep time: 5 minutes. Cooking: 20 minutes on high.
Suitable for: LF, LC, VGI, VGN, PC, WD.

Ingredients:
- ½ pound taro, washed
- ½ Tbsp sesame seed oil
- 1 tsp soy sauce
- 1 tsp oyster sauce

Directions:
1. Using a mandolin, slice the taro thinly.
2. Rinse the slices and pat dry.
3. Coat with oil and the oyster and soy sauces. Place in air fryer.
4. Cook at 400F for 20 minutes.

Nutritional values per serving: KCAL: 80; net C 12g; P 2g; F 2g.
Serve as-is.

Air Fried Cassava Croquettes.

Serves 4. Prep time: 5 minutes. Cooking: 5 minutes on high.
Suitable for: LC, LF, VGI, VGN, PC.

Ingredients:
- 1 pound thick cassava porridge
- ½ cup breadcrumbs
- 1 kcal spray
- salt, pepper, sugar

Directions:
1. Create cassava porridge balls in bite-size pieces.
2. Mix cassava balls with the salt, pepper, and sugar.
3. Roll the pieces in breadcrumbs. Spray with oil. Place in air fryer.
4. Cook at 340F for 9 minutes.
5. Season with salt.

Nutritional values per serving: KCAL: 140; net C 31g; P 2g; F 1g.
Serve as a side dish.

Air Fried Sweet Potato Chips.

Serves 2. Prep time: 5 minutes. Cooking: 20 minutes on high.
Suitable for: LF, LC, PL, VGI, VGN, PC, WD.

Ingredients:
- ½ pound sweet potatoes
- ½ Tbsp olive oil
- Pinch of salt
- Pinch of sugar

Directions:
1. Using a mandolin, slice the sweet potatoes into thin pieces, ¼ inch thickness.
2. Rinse the slices in cold water until water runs clear. Pat dry.
3. Coat with oil and salt. Place in air fryer.

4. Cook at 400F for 20 minutes.
5. Season with sugar.

Nutritional values per serving: KCAL: 130; net C 40g; P 2g; F 2g. Serve as-is.

Air Fried Falafel.

Serves 4. Prep time: 5 minutes. Cooking: 5 minutes on high.
Suitable for: LC, LF, VGI, VGN, PC.

Ingredients:
- 1 pound cooked chickpeas
- handful oats
- handful minced vegetables
- 1 kcal spray
- 1 tsp Turkish spice blend

Directions:
1. Mix chickpeas, oats, vegetables, and spices.
2. Roll into bite-size balls. Spray with oil. Place in air fryer.
3. Cook at 340F for 9 minutes.
4. Season with salt.

Nutritional values per serving: KCAL: 82; net C 13g; P 5g; F 1g. Serve as a side dish.

Air Fried Bean Chips.

Serves 2. Prep time: 5 minutes. Cooking: 40 minutes on low.
Suitable for: LF, VGI, VGN, PC, WD.

Ingredients:
- ½ pound drained tinned beans
- ½ Tbsp olive oil
- salt

Directions:
1. Mash the beans. Add oil and salt.
2. Form flat discs, dry out. Drizzle oil along bottom of air fryer.
3. Cook at 320F for 40 minutes.

Nutritional values per serving: KCAL: 100; net C 17g; P 2g; F 2g.
Serve as-is.

Air Fried Lentil Balls.

Serves 4. Prep time: 5 minutes. Cooking: 5 minutes on high.
Suitable for: LC, LF, VGI, VGN, PC.

Ingredients:
- 1 pound cooked red lentils
- ½ cup breadcrumbs
- 1 kcal spray
- Pinch of salt
- Pinch of garlic powder

Directions:
1. Mix the lentils, salt, and garlic powder together. Roll into bite-size balls.
2. Spray with oil. Roll in breadcrumbs. Spray with oil again. Place in air fryer.
3. Cook at 340F for 9 minutes.
4. Season with salt.

Nutritional values per serving: KCAL: 95; net C 17g; P 7g; F 1g.
Serve as a side dish.

Air Fried Rice Balls.

Serves 5. Prep time: 30 minutes. Cooking: 10 minutes on low/medium/high. Suitable for: LC, LF, VGI, PC.

Ingredients:
- ½ cup risotto
- 1 cup mixed diced vegetables
- ¼ cup vegetable stock
- ½ cup flour
- 1 egg, beaten
- 1 cup breadcrumbs
- 1 kcal spray
- Pinch of salt and pepper

Directions:
1. Cook the risotto in the vegetable stock.
2. Mash the risotto with vegetables.
3. Roll mixture into bite-size balls.
4. Dip the ball in flour, then egg, then breadcrumbs.
5. Spray with oil. Place in air fryer.
6. Cook at 400F for 5 minutes.

Nutritional values per serving: KCAL: 190; net C 36g; P 3g; F 6g. Serve as-is.

Air Fried Corn Balls.

Serves 5. Prep time: 30 minutes. Cooking: 10 minutes on low/medium/high. Suitable for: LC, LF, VGI, PC.

Ingredients:
- 1 pound sweetcorn, blended
- ¼ cup flour
- 1 egg

- 1 cup breadcrumbs
- 1 kcal spray
- salt and pepper
- Mexican papas bravas blend

Directions:
1. Add the seasoning, salt, and pepper to the corn. Mash together.
2. Roll mixture into bite-size balls. Then dip in flour, egg, then breadcrumbs.
3. Spray with oil. Place in air fryer.
4. Cook at 400F for 5 minutes.

Nutritional values per serving: *KCAL: 100; net C 19g; P 3g; F 6g.*
Serve with dipping sauce.

Chapter 9: Fruits & Vegetables

Often we shy away from frying fruits and vegetables, for obvious reasons. Quite simply: if we are going to try and eat healthy, then surely the last thing on our minds should be frying plants in fattening, processed oils? It sort of defeats the point. But with an air-fryer you can make tasty, crispy "fried" fruit and vegetables, often without any oil at all, for very little effort.

Air Fried Eggplant Parmesan Fries.

Serves 3. Prep time: 10 minutes. Cooking: 20 minutes on high.
Suitable for: LC, LF, VGI, PC, WD.

Ingredients:
- 1 pound eggplant
- 2 large egg whites
- ½ cup flour
- 1 tsp garlic powder
- ½ cup breadcrumbs
- ½ cup grated parmesan cheese
- 1 kcal spray
- Pinch of salt and pepper

Directions:
1. Cut eggplant into sticks. Pat dry.
2. Mix flour with garlic powder. Mix breadcrumbs with parmesan cheese.
3. Beat egg whites with salt and pepper.
4. Dip sticks in flour, then eggs, then breadcrumbs. Repeat for cruncher crust.
5. Spray with oil. Place in air fryer.
6. Cook 350F for 20 minutes.

Nutritional values per serving: KCAL: 80; net C 8g; P 3g; F 3g.
Serve with dipping sauce, or as a side dish.

Air Fried Savoy Coconut Lime Chips.

Serves 5. Prep time: 1 minute. Cooking: 2 minutes on high.
Suitable for: KD, LC, LF, AK, PL, VGI, VGN, PC, WD.

Ingredients:
- 1 medium head of savoy cabbage
- 1 Tbsp sesame, coconut, or olive oil
- 1 tsp coconut flakes
- 1 tsp lime juice

Directions:
1. Remove centre stem of savoy cabbage. Rinse leaves and pat dry.
2. Tear or chop into even-ish squares.
3. Coat in oil. Place in air fryer.
4. Cook at 400F for 2 minutes.
5. Splash with lime and sprinkle with coconut.

Nutritional values per serving: KCAL: 48; net C 2g; P 0g; F 5g.
Serve with a dip, or as a side dish.

Air Fried Brussel Sprouts.

Serves 2. Prep time: 5 minutes. Cooking:10 minutes on high.
Suitable for: LC, AK, PL, VGI, VGN, PC, WD.

Ingredients:
- 1 pound brussel sprouts, chopped
- 1 Tbsp olive oil
- Pinch of salt and pepper
- 2 – 4 Tbsp balsamic reduction

Directions:
1. Toss brussel sprouts in oil, balsamic reduction, salt, and pepper.
2. Place in air fryer.
3. Cook at 400F for 10 minutes.

Nutritional values per serving: KCAL: 100; net C 15g; P 4g; F g12.
Serve as-is.

Air Fried Banana Chips.

Serves 6. Prep time: 15 minutes. Cooking: 15 minutes on high.
Suitable for: LF, VGI, VGN, PC, WD.

Ingredients:
- 4 bananas, sliced in rings
- 2 Tbsp corn starch or rice flour
- 1 tsp olive oil
- salt and pepper

Directions:
1. Slice the banana into thin rings.
2. Dip banana slices in corn starch or rice flour. Let rest for 10 minutes, to dry.
3. Toss the pieces in oil. Place the slices in the air fryer.
4. Cook at 375F for 15 minutes.

Nutritional values per serving: KCAL: 100; net C 20g; P 2g; F 2g.
Serve with a nice dip, or as a simple snack.

Air Fried Pumpkin Spice Fries.

Serves 3. Prep time: 10 minutes. Cooking: 20 minutes on high.
Suitable for: LC, LF, VGI, PC.

Ingredients:
- 1 pound pumpkin or similar squash
- 2 large egg whites
- ½ cup flour

- 1 tsp cinnamon
- 1 tsp sugar
- 1 tsp nutmeg
- ½ cup breadcrumbs from pastry or cake
- 1 kcal spray
- salt and pepper

Directions:
1. Cut pumpkin into sticks. Pat dry.
2. Beat egg whites with salt and pepper.
3. Dip sticks into flour, then eggs, then breadcrumbs. Repeat for crunchier crust.
4. Spray with oil. Place in air fryer.
5. Cook at 350F for 20 minutes.

Nutritional values per serving: *KCAL: 150; net C 20g; P 3g; F 7g.*
Serve with dipping sauce, or as a side dish.

Air Fried Sesame Broccoli.

Serves 2. Prep time: 5 minutes. Cooking:10 minutes on high.
Suitable for: LC, AK, VGI, VGN, PC, WD.

Ingredients:
- 1 pound broccoli florets
- 1 Tbsp sesame seed oil
- Pinch of salt and pepper
- sesame seeds

Directions:
1. Chop into florets. Rinse and pat dry.
2. Toss florets in sesame seed oil. Season with salt and pepper.
3. Place in air fryer.
4. Cook at 400F for 10 minutes.

Nutritional values per serving: *KCAL: 120; net C 15g; P 4g; F g17.*
Serve as-is.

Air Fried Pak Choi Chips.

Serves 5. Prep time: 1 minute. Cooking: 2 minutes on high.
Suitable for: KD, LC, LF, AK, PL, VGI, VGN, PC, WD.

Ingredients:
- 3 pak choi cabbages
- 3 - 4 Tbsp sesame seed oil
- 1 tsp 5 spice

Directions:
1. Remove centre stem of each pak choi.
2. Rinse leaves and pat dry.
3. Tear or chop into even-ish squares.
4. Coat in oil. Place in air fryer.
5. Cook at 400F for 2 minutes.
6. Season with spices.

Nutritional values per serving: *KCAL: 17; net C 2g; P 0g; F 1g.*
Serve with a dip, or as a side dish.

Air Fried Apple Rings And Bits.

Serves 6. Prep time: 15 minutes. Cooking: 15 minutes on high.
Suitable for: LF, VGI, VGN, PC, WD.

Ingredients:
- 4 apples, peeled, cored, sliced
- 2 Tbsp corn starch or rice starch
- 1 tsp olive oil
- sugar and cinnamon

Directions:
1. In a baggie, combine the starch or rice flour, sugar, and cinnamon.
2. Add the apple slices. Toss to coat evenly. Leave 10 minutes to settle.

3. Coat in oil. Place in air fryer.
4. Cook at 350F for 15 minutes.

Nutritional values per serving: KCAL: 100; net C 20g; P 2g; F 2g.
Serve as-is.

Air Fried Sweet Potato Fries.

Serves 3. Prep time: 10 minutes. Cooking: 20 minutes on high.
Suitable for: LC, LF, VGI, PC, WD.

Ingredients:
- 1 pound sweet potatoes
- 2 large egg whites
- ½ cup flour
- 1 tsp salt
- 1 tsp onion powder
- ½ cup breadcrumbs
- 1 tsp chili flakes
- 1 kcal spray

Directions:
1. Peel sweet potatoes and cut into sticks. Pat dry.
2. Beat egg whites with salt and pepper.
3. Dip sticks into flour, then eggs, then crumbs. Repeat for crunchier crust.
4. Spray pieces with oil. Place in air fryer.
5. Cook at 350F for 20 minutes.

Nutritional values per serving: KCAL: 200; net C 36g; P 1g; F 6g.
Serve with dipping sauce, or as a side dish.

Air Fried Artichoke Hearts.

Serves 2. Prep time: 5 minutes. Cooking: 10 minutes on high.
Suitable for: LC, AK, PL, VGI, VGN, PC, WD.

Ingredients:
- 1 pound quartered artichoke hearts
- 1 Tbsp olive oil
- salt and pepper
- garlic paste

Directions:
1. Toss artichokes in oil. Season with salt, pepper, and garlic paste.
2. Place in air fryer.
3. Cook at 400F for 10 minutes.

Nutritional values per serving: KCAL: 100; net C 17g; P 2g; F g12.
Serve as-is.

Air Fried Coconut Chips.

Serves 8. Prep time: 15 minutes. Cooking: 25 minutes on high.
Suitable for: KD, LC, AK, VGI, VGN, PC, WD.

Ingredients:
- 1 coconut, shelled and washed
- 2 Tbsp corn starch or rice flour
- 1 tsp olive oil
- salt

Directions:
1. Using a mandolin, slice the coconut into thin slices.
2. Coat in oil. Season with salt.
3. Dip in corn starch or rice flour. Place in air fryer.
4. Cook at 400F for 25 minutes.

Nutritional values per serving: KCAL: 190; net C 7g; P 2g; F 16g.
Serve as-is.

Air Fried Onion Rings.

Serves 2. Prep time: 5 minutes. Cooking: 10 minutes on high.
Suitable for: LC, AK, VGI, VGN, PC.

Ingredients:
- 1 pound onions, sliced in rings
- 1 cup breadcrumbs
- 1 kcal spray
- salt and pepper

Directions:
1. Slice onions into ½ inch thickness. Pat dry.
2. Mix the breadcrumbs with salt and pepper.
3. Spray with oil. Dip slices in breadcrumbs mixture. Place in air fryer.
4. Cook at 400F for 10 minutes.

Nutritional values per serving: KCAL: 130; net C 15g; P 4g; F g21.
Serve as-is.

Air Fried Buffalo Cauliflower.

Serves 2. Prep time: 10 minutes. Cooking: 15 minutes on low.
Suitable for: LC, VGI, VGN, PC.

Ingredients:
- 1 large cauliflower head, cut into florets
- 1 cup breadcrumbs
- ¼ cup melted margarine (melt margarine until you have ¼ cup)
- ¼ cup buffalo sauce
- salt

Directions:
1. Mix the margarine and buffalo sauce.
2. Pour the margarine and buffalo sauce mix into a large baggie.

3. Add the florets. Massage until they are evenly coated.
4. Dip the florets in breadcrumbs. Place in air fryer.
5. Cook at 325F for 15 minutes.

Nutritional values per serving: *KCAL: 400; net C 36g; P 12g; F 20g.*
Serve as a side dish, or with a salad and dip.

Air Fried Spicy Mango Chips.

Serves 6. Prep time: 15 minutes. Cooking: 60 minutes on low.
Suitable for: LF, VGI, VGN, PC, WD.

Ingredients:
- 1 large mango, thinly sliced mandolin
- 1 tsp olive oil
- salt and pepper
- 1 tsp cayenne pepper
- 1 tsp paprika

Directions:
1. In a large baggie, pour in the cayenne pepper, paprika, salt, and pepper.
2. Toss in mango slices. Massage to coat evenly.
3. Set aside 10 minutes for seasoning to settle.
4. Coat in oil. Place in air fryer.
5. Cook at 325F for 60 minutes.

Nutritional values per serving: *KCAL: 130; net C 25g; P 2g; F 2g.*
Serve as-is.

Air Fried Beet Fries.

Serves 3. Prep time: 10 minutes. Cooking: 20 minutes on high.
Suitable for: LC, LF, VGI, PC, WD.

Ingredients:
- 1 pound peeled, boiled beets
- 2 large egg whites
- ½ cup flour
- Pinch of salt
- Pinch of sugar
- ½ cup breadcrumbs
- 1 tsp herbes du provence
- 1 kcal spray

Directions:
1. Cut beets into sticks. Pat dry.
2. Beat egg whites with salt and pepper.
3. Dip sticks into flour, then eggs, then breadcrumbs. Repeat for crunchier crust.
4. Spray with oil. Place in air fryer.
5. Cook at 350F for 20 minutes.

Nutritional values per serving: KCAL: 130; net C 21g; P 3g; F 4g.
Serve with sauce for dipping, or as a side dish.

Chapter 10: Vegan & Vegetarian

A lot of amazing vegan and vegetarian snacks are also really bad for us. This is, of course, true for many snacks enjoyed by meat-eaters, as well. It seems as though the best, healthiest snacks are often either unethical, or made out of animal products. However, when we air-fry our food, we can make delicious meat-free, ethical dishes right at home. Perfect!

Air Fried Maple Sprouts.

Serves 2. Prep time: 5 minutes. Cooking: 10 minutes on high.
Suitable for: LC, AK, PL, VGI, VGN, PC, WD.

Ingredients:
- 1 pound brussel sprouts, chopped
- 1 Tbsp olive oil
- Pinch of salt and pepper
- 1 -2 Tbsp maple syrup

Directions:
1. Toss brussel sprouts in maple syrup. Season with salt and pepper.
2. Drizzle oil over bottom of air fryer. Place sprouts in air fryer.
3. Cook at 400F for 10 minutes.

Nutritional values per serving: KCAL: 90; net C 25g; P 4g; F 3g.
Serve as-is.

Air Fried Cheesy Acorn Squash Fries.

Serves 3. Prep time: 10 minutes. Cooking: 20 minutes on high.
Suitable for: LC, LF, VGI, PC, WD.

Ingredients:
- 1 pound acorn squash
- 2 large egg whites
- ½ cup flour

- Pinch of salt
- 1 tsp paprika
- ½ cup breadcrumbs
- 1 tsp parmesan cheese
- 1 kcal spray
- grated cheeses, 1-5 varieties

Directions:
1. Peel and deseed squash. Cut into sticks. Pat dry.
2. Beat egg whites with salt and pepper.
3. Dip sticks in flour, then eggs, then breadcrumbs. Repeat for crunchier crust.
4. Spray with oil. Place in air fryer.
5. Cook at 350F for 20 minutes.
6. Melt cheese on top once cooked.

Nutritional values per serving: KCAL: 110; net C 12g; P 3g; F 4g. Serve with dipping sauce, or as a side dish.

Air Fried Spring Rolls.

Serves 4. Prep time: 15 minutes. Cooking: 25 minutes on high. Suitable for: LC, LF, AK, VGI, VGN, PC.

Ingredients:
- 8 spring roll sheets
- 2 cups shredded cabbage
- 1 cup shredded onion
- 1 carrot, shredded
- 2 Tbsp garlic paste
- 2 Tbsp ginger paste
- salt, sugar, and pepper
- 1 kcal spray

Directions:
1. Mix the vegetables. Stir in the pastes.

2. Place the ingredients in middle of spring roll, wrap tightly. Use water to seal.
3. Spray the roll with oil to coat evenly. Place in air fryer.
4. Cook at 350F for 25 minutes.

Nutritional values per serving: KCAL: 108; net C 15g; P 3g; F 4g.
Serve with a dipping sauce and a salad.

Air Fried Garlic Cauliflower.

Serves 2. Prep time: 10 minutes. Cooking: 15 minutes on low.
Suitable for: LC, VGI, VGN, PC.

Ingredients:
- 1 large cauliflower head, cut into florets
- 1 cup breadcrumbs
- ¼ cup melted margarine
- ¼ cup garlic paste
- 2 Tbsp soy sauce
- salt

Directions:
1. In a bowl, mix the margarine, soy sauce, and garlic paste.
2. Dip florets in sauce mix, then breadcrumbs. Sprinkle with salt. Place in air fryer.
3. Cook at 325F for 15 minutes.

Nutritional values per serving: KCAL: 250; net C 24g; P 12g; F 18g.
Serve as a side dish, or with a salad and dip.

Air Fried Papas Bravas.

Serves 3. Prep time: 10 minutes. Cooking: 20 minutes on high.
Suitable for: LC, LF, VGI, PC, WD.

Ingredients:

- 1 pound medium-sized, white or red potatoes
- 2 large egg whites
- ½ cup flour
- ½ cup
- 1 tsp smoked paprika
- 1 tsp cayenne pepper
- 1 tsp salt
- 1 tsp garlic powder
- Pinch of saffron
- 1 kcal spray

Directions:

1. Cut potatoes into sticks. Pat dry.
2. Beat egg whites with salt and pepper.
3. Mix breadcrumbs with paprika, cayenne pepper, salt, garlic powder, saffron.
4. Dip sticks in flour, then eggs, then breadcrumbs. Repeat for crunchier crust.
5. Spray with oil, coat evenly. Place in air fryer.
6. Cook at 350F for 20 minutes.

Nutritional values per serving: *KCAL: 170; net C 34g; P 3g; F 4g.*
Serve with dipping sauce, or as a side dish.

Air Fried Red Bean Burger.

Serves 6. Prep time: 15 minutes. Cooking: 25 minutes on high.
Suitable for: LC, LF, VGI, VGN, PC, WD.

Ingredients:

- 2 cans kidney beans, drained
- 1 cup minced carrot
- ½ cup minced onions
- 1 Tbsp tomato paste
- Pinch of herbes du provence
- salt and pepper

- ½ cup flour
- oil

Directions:
1. Mash all ingredients together.
2. Form 6 patties. Roll in flour.
3. Drizzle oil over bottom of air fryer. Place patties in air fryer.
4. Cook at 350F for 25 minutes.

Nutritional values per serving: KCAL: 125; net C 32g; P 12g; F 3g. Serve on a bun with salad.

Air Fried Roast Potatoes.

Serves 3. Prep time: 10 minutes. Cooking: 25 minutes on high. Suitable for: LC, VGI, VGN, PC, WD.

Ingredients:
- 1.5 pound red potatoes
- 1 Tbsp rice flour
- 1 Tbsp papas bravas spices
- 1 Tbsp garlic powder
- salt and pepper
- oil

Directions:
1. Mix seasonings and flour in a bowl.
2. Chop potatoes roughly. Boil until el dante.
3. Pat dry and coat with seasoned flour.
4. Drizzle oil over bottom of air fryer. Place in air fryer.
5. Cook at 350F for 25 minutes.

Nutritional values per serving: KCAL: 165; net C 35g; P 4g; F 12g. Serve with aioli for dipping.

Air Fried Spinach and Feta Croquettes.

Serves 4. Prep time: 10 minutes. Cooking: 7 minutes on high.
Suitable for: LC, LF, VGI, PC, WD.

Ingredients:
- ½ pound feta, minced
- 1 cup spinach, washed, dried, finely chopped
- ½ cup potatoes, mashed
- 1 Tbsp butter
- 1 – 2 Tbsp milk
- ½ cup breadcrumbs
- 2 eggs, beaten
- Pinch of salt and pepper
- Pinch of onion powder.
- ⅓ cup oil

Directions:
1. Mash the cooked potatoes with milk and butter.
2. Roll into bite-size balls.
3. Mix the feta and spinach.
4. Mix the breadcrumbs with salt and pepper, onion powder.
5. Make a pocket in each ball and insert the filling.
6. Roll in flour, then egg, then breadcrumbs.
7. Drizzle oil over bottom of air fryer. Place balls in air fryer.
8. Cook at 400F for 7 minutes. In small batches, so they don't stick.

Nutritional values per serving: KCAL: 200; net C 24g; P 11g; F 9g.
Serve with dipping sauce.

Air Fried Swede Fries.

Serves 3. Prep time: 10 minutes. Cooking: 20 minutes on high.
Suitable for: KD, LC, LF, VGI, PC, WD.

Ingredients:
- 1 pound swede
- 2 large egg whites
- ½ cup flour
- 1 tsp onion powder
- Pinch of fresh ground black pepper
- 1 kcal spray
-

Directions:
1. Cut swede into sticks. Pat dry.
2. Pre-boil or steam in microwave to soften. Dry again.
3. Beat egg whites with salt and pepper.
4. Dip sticks into eggs, then flour. Repeat for crunchier crust.
5. Spray with oil, coat evenly. Place in air fryer.
6. Cook at 250F for 20 minutes.

Nutritional values per serving: KCAL: 95; net C 6g; P 3g; F 4g.
Serve with sauce for dipping, or as a side dish.

Air Fried 5 Spice Broccoli.

Serves 2. Prep time: 5 minutes. Cooking: 10 minutes on high.
Suitable for: LC, AK, PL, VGI, VGN, PC, WD.

Ingredients:
- 1 pound chopped broccoli
- 1 Tbsp olive oil
- salt and pepper
- 5 spice (star anise, cloves, Chinese cinnamon, Sichuan pepper, fennel seeds)

Directions:
1. Cut broccoli into florets. Place florets in a baggie. Add the oil, salt, pepper, and spice mix. Massage to coat evenly.
2. Place in air fryer.

3. Cook at 400F for 10 minutes.

Nutritional values per serving: KCAL: 90; net C 11g; P 4g; F g12.
Serve as-is.

Air Fried Avocado Fries.

Serves 4. Prep time: 10 minutes. Cooking: 10 minutes on high.
Suitable for: LC, AK, VGI, VGN, PC, WD.

Ingredients:
- 1 large avocado
- ½ cup breadcrumbs
- salt and pepper
- 1 kcal spray

Directions:
1. Mix breadcrumbs with salt and pepper.
2. Peel, stone, and slice your avocado. Spray the avocado with oil.
3. Dip avocado slices in breadcrumbs. Place in air fryer.
4. Cook at 400F for 10 minutes.

Nutritional values per serving: KCAL: 300; net C 24g; P 5g; F 20g.
Serve with a hot dipping sauce.

Air Fried Pizza Croquettes.

Serves 4. Prep time: 10 minutes. Cooking: 7 minutes on high.
Suitable for: LC, VGI, PC, WD.

Ingredients:
- 1 cup tomato sauce
- ½ cup mozzarella cheese
- ½ cup diced vegetables

- ½ cup breadcrumbs
- ¼ cup flour
- 2 eggs, beaten
- ⅓ cup oil

Directions:
1. Mix the bread crumbs with salt and pepper and eggs. (If mixture is too wet, add more breadcrumbs.)
2. Form bite-size balls.
3. Filling: Mix the tomato sauce, vegetables, and cheese.
4. Make a pocket in each ball and insert the filling.
5. Roll in flour.
6. Drizzle oil over bottom of air fryer. Place pizza croquettes in air fryer.
7. Cook at 400F for 7 minutes. In small batches, so they don't stick.

Nutritional values per serving: KCAL: 340; net C 27g; P 13g; F 25g.
Serve with marinara or pizza sauce.

Air Fried Crispy Tofu.

Serves 4. Prep time: 35 minutes. Cooking: 20 minutes on high.
Suitable for: HP, LC, LF, AK, VGI, VGN, PC.
Ingredients:
- 1 cup firm tofu, cubed
- 2 Tbsp soy sauce
- 2 Tbsp sesame seed oil
- 1 tsp rice wine vinegar

Directions:
1. In a baggie, combine the tofu, soy sauce, sesame oil, and rice wine vinegar.
2. Massage tofu through bag until evenly coated. Let it rest for 30 minutes.
3. Place in air fryer.
4. Cook at 350F for 20 minutes.

Nutritional values per serving: KCAL: 180; net C 15g; P 23g; F 4g.
Serve as-is.

Air Fried Onion Bhajis.

Serves 2. Prep time: 5 minutes. Cooking: 15 minutes on high.
Suitable for: LC, LF, VGI, VGN, PC, WD.

Ingredients:
- 1 large Spanish onion, thinly sliced
- ½ cup flour
- 1 Tbsp coriander
- ¼ Tbsp cumin
- Dash of salt and pepper
- 1 – 2 Tbsp water, as needed
- 1 kcal spray

Directions:
1. In a bowl, combine flour, onion, coriander, cumin, salt, pepper.
2. Drizzle in water. Stir until smooth.
3. Make batter cakes. Spray with kcal oil. Place in air fryer.
4. Cook at 350F for 15 minutes.

Nutritional values per serving: KCAL: 130; net C 17g; P 12g; F 8g.
Serve as-is.

Air Fried Artichokes In Tomato.

Serves 2. Prep time: 5 minutes. Cooking: 10 minutes on high.
Suitable for: LC, AK, PL, VGI, VGN, PC, WD.

Ingredients:
- 1 pound artichokes, chopped
- 1 Tbsp olive oil
- Pinch of salt and pepper
- 3 Tbsp tomato paste

- oil

Directions:
1. Toss chopped artichokes with the tomato paste, salt, and pepper.
2. Drizzle oil over bottom of air fryer. Place artichokes in air fryer.
3. Cook at 350F for 10 minutes.

Nutritional values per serving: *KCAL: 130; net C 25g; P 4g; F g12.*
Serve as-is.

Chapter 11: 4 Week Meal Planner

When it comes to starting out with a new kitchen gadget, a new diet, or both at the same time, it is easy to fall off the wagon and go back to your old way of eating. This is because it takes up to thirty days to develop a new habit. So, the more help you get over those first four weeks, the better, right?

This meal planner should help you to follow a healthy, air fryer diet for four weeks, making it easier to incorporate these great recipes into your everyday life. The idea behind the planner is that you will buy all your ingredients at the start and only top up shop on fresh ingredients. You will also cook something, then you may eat it for several days in a row before making something else. Otherwise, reduce the amount in the recipe to match your needs. Air fried food do not freeze well, so you will need to be careful about how much you cook and when you cook it.

This meal planner also assumes you have no special dietary requirements. If you do have special dietary requirements, then you will need to create your own meal plan. Use this planner as inspiration to build your perfect four weeks.

Every recipe has letters next to it indicating which diet it is suitable for, so just skip through until you spot something you like, then add it to the list!

Shopping List

CARBS	PROTEIN	DAIRY	FRUITS	VEG	SPICES	FATS
-flour -gram flour -rice flour -7oz puff pastry -2 cups breadcrumbs -6lbs potatoes	-34 eggs -46 rashers bacon -4 sausages -2lb turkey -1lb shrimp 2lbs lamb -1.5lbs sausage -14oz firm tofu -16 chicken wings -2 6oz steaks	-2tbsp milk -1/2lb feta -1 tin coconut milk	-5 tomatoes -1 eggplant -1 zucchini	-5 cups button mushrooms -head of cabbage-4 large onions -7oz spinach -1 cauliflower head -1lb brussel sprouts	-maple syrup -madras paste -curry powder -garlic paste -coriander -cumin -soy sauce -rice vinegar -salt -pepper	-1kcal spray -sesame oil -sunflower oil -olive oil -margarine

Week 1

	MON	TUE	WED	THU	FRI	SAT	SUN
Breakfast	Maple bacon and eggs.	Croissant.	Maple bacon and eggs.	Croissant.	Maple bacon and eggs.	Croissant.	Maple bacon and eggs.
Lunch	Turkey and mushroom burgers.	Crispy tofu. French fries.	Turkey and mushroom burgers. French fries.	Crispy tofu. French fries.	Turkey and mushroom burgers.	Spicy curry wings.	Shrimp patties. French fries.
Dinner	Onion bhajis. Crispy tofu.	Turkey and mushroom burgers. French fries.	Onion bhajis. Crispy tofu.	Turkey and mushroom burgers.	Spicy curry wings.	Shrimp patties. French fries.	Spicy curry wings.

Week 2

	MON	TUE	WED	THU	FRI	SAT	SUN
Breakfast	Croissant.	Maple bacon and eggs.	Croissant.	Maple bacon and eggs.	Croissant.	Maple bacon and eggs.	Croissant.
Lunch	Spicy curry. wings.	Shrimp patties. French fries.	Spinach and feta. croquettes.	Crispy meatballs. French fries.	Spinach and feta. croquettes.	Crispy meatballs. French fries.	Spinach and feta. croquettes.
Dinner	Shrimp patties. French fries.	Spinach and feta. croquettes.	Shrimp patties. French fries.	Onion bhajis.	Crispy meatballs. French fries.	Onion bhajis.	Crispy meatballs. French fries.

Week 3

	MON	TUE	WED	THU	FRI	SAT	SUN
Breakfast	Maple bacon and eggs.	Croissant.	Maple bacon and eggs.	Breakfast skewer.	Maple bacon and eggs.	Breakfast skewer.	Maple bacon and eggs.
Lunch	Crispy meatballs. French fries.	Garlic cauliflower.	Crispy meatballs. French fries.	Turkey and mushroom burgers.	Crispy tofu. French fries.	Turkey and mushroom burgers. French fries.	Maple sprouts.
Dinner	Garlic cauliflower.	Crispy meatballs. French fries.	Onion bhajis. Crispy tofu.	Onion bhajis. Crispy tofu.	Turkey and mushroom burgers. French fries.	Crispy tofu. French fries.	Turkey and mushroom burgers. French fries.

Week 4

	MON	TUE	WED	THU	FRI	SAT	SUN
Breakfast	Breakfast skewer.	Maple bacon and eggs.	Breakfast skewer.	Maple bacon and eggs.	Breakfast skewer.	Maple bacon and eggs.	Breakfast skewer.
Lunch	Turkey and mushroom burgers. French fries.	Onion bhajis.	Spicy lamb curry.	French fries.	Spicy lamb curry.	Steak and eggs.	Spicy lamb curry.
Dinner	Maple sprouts.	Spicy lamb curry.	Onion bhajis.	Spicy lamb curry.	French fries.	Spicy lamb curry.	Steak and eggs.

Conclusion

An air fryer can be a confusing, complicated kitchen gadget for a new user. However, throughout this book you should have gained new knowledge and experience, giving you the confidence to use your air fryer regularly at home. This excellent choice means that now you can enjoy delicious fried foods in a healthier way. All you need to do just put it into action! Good luck!

Made in the USA
San Bernardino, CA
10 January 2018